Sonlight + D
Binny B

P9-EAJ-543

———— THE BEGINNER'S ————

# AMERICAN HISTORY

FROM CHRISTOPHER COLUMBUS TO JOHN SUTTER

## D.H. MONTGOMERY

EDITED AND UPDATED BY JOHN A. HOLZMANN

Avyx

Published by Avyx, Inc., Littleton, Colorado, U.S.A.

Revised text, including prefatory note, index and maps on pages 3, 4, 41, 61, and 76 created by Dave Lilly and copyright © 2014 Avyx, Inc.

Cover design by Cassi Gloe

The original version of The Beginner's American History was published in 1893 by Ginn & Company, Boston, Massachusetts.

D.H. Montgomery (David Henry)

The Beginner's American History

ISBN: 978-1-935570-18-9

LCCN: 2013953476

Manufactured in the United States of America

D.H.M
to
S.K.K.

**Prefatory Note**

This little book is intended to present clearly and accurately those facts and principles in the lives of some of the chief founders and builders of America which would be of interest and value to pupils beginning the study of our history. I have taken great care to relate only such incidents and anecdotes as are believed to rest on good authority.

The numerous illustrations in the text are, in nearly every case, from drawings and designs made by Miss C. S. King of Boston.

David H. Montgomery,

Cambridge, Mass.

# Table of Contents

# Author's Note

I provided the paragraph headings to give you topical references. I thought you might also modify them slightly to create comprehension questions. If you ignore these headings, you can use the book as a reader.

If you want regular questions, you will find them at the end of each section. You will find difficult words defined or pronounced in footnotes where they first occur. You can also find references to them in the index.

# Christopher Columbus
1436-1506[1]

## Birth and boyhood of Columbus

Christopher Columbus was born at Genoa[2] more than 450 years ago. Genoa was a seaport in Italy. Christopher's father was a wool-comber.[3] Christopher did not care to learn that trade. He wanted to become a sailor. Seeing the boy's strong interest in the sea, his father sent him to a school where he could learn geography, map-drawing, and whatever else might help him to become commander of a vessel.

Columbus as a boy.

From the statue in the Museum of Fine Arts, Boston.

## Columbus becomes a sailor

When he was 14, Columbus went to sea. In those days, the Mediterranean Sea[4] swarmed with war-ships and pirates. Every sailor—even boys—had to stand ready to fight from port to port.

Columbus grew to manhood in the middle of this kind of exciting life, full of adventure and danger. The rough experiences he

---

1  These dates under a name show the year the person was born and died.
2  Genoa (Jen'o-ah); see Map 5, p. 16.
3  Wool-comber: Before sheep's wool can be spun into thread and woven into cloth, it must be combed out straight and smooth. Men who did this were called wool-combers. They combed the wool by hand.
4  Mediterranean (Med'i-ter-ra'ne-an) means "middle of the earth." Mediterranean Sea, then, is "the sea at the middle of the earth." And that's the way the leading cultures of that time viewed it. Everything of importance in the world happened right there in the Mediterranean.

had helped to make him the brave, determined captain he would become later.

## Columbus has a sea-fight; he goes to Lisbon

According to some accounts, Columbus was once part of the crew on a ship that entered into desperate battle with another vessel. They were about six miles off the coast of Portugal. The fight lasted all day. Eventually, both ships burst into flames. Columbus jumped from his ship into the sea. He grabbed a floating oar and began swimming toward the shore all those miles away!

He made it to shore. He then traveled to the port of Lisbon.[5] While there, he met and eventually married the daughter of a famous sea captain. For a long time after, Columbus supported his family by means of two trades. 1) He drew maps and then sold them to commanders of ships that were visiting Lisbon. 2) He also continued to sail and made a number of voyages to Africa, Iceland, and other countries.

## What people then knew about the world

The maps that Columbus made and sold were very different from those we have today. At that time, less than half of the world as we know it had been discovered. Europe, Asia, and a small part of Africa were the chief countries people in the Mediterranean knew about.

Columbus' maps may have shown the earth shaped like a ball, but he thought it was much smaller than we know it really is. No one had sailed around the globe at that time. No one knew that other lands lay west of the Atlantic. They thought that the Atlantic (on the west side of Europe) and

---

5   Lisbon: see Map 5, p. 16.

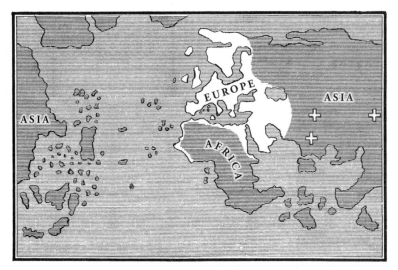

Map 1. The light parts of this map show how much of the world was then well-known; the white crosses show those parts of Eastern Asia of which something was known. You can see how far Columbus imagined his trip to Asia might be.

the Pacific (on the east side of Asia) were one ocean. Most seamen thought it was a huge ocean—far too large to ever sail across. For this reason, if we were to see one of the maps Columbus drew, we would look in vain for the great continents of North and South America. We wouldn't find Australia, either.

## Columbus' plan to reach the Indies by sailing west

While living in Lisbon, Columbus made up his mind to try to do what no other man had dared attempt. He would try to cross the Atlantic Ocean. He thought that, by going west, he could get directly to Asia and the Indies. He believed they were directly opposite Portugal and Spain. If his voyage was successful, he could open up a very profitable trade with the rich countries of the East. These countries had spices, drugs, and silk for which people in Europe were willing to pay high prices.

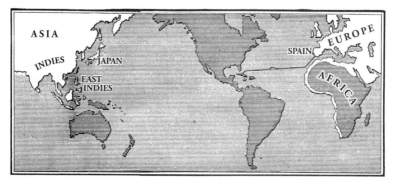

Map 2. This map shows how Columbus' trip actually turned out. He had no idea that America lay in the way. Nor did he know how tremendously far he would have had to travel if the Americas had not been in the way!

For over two hundred years, Europeans had purchased these goods. The goods passed through the lands on the eastern edge of the Mediterranean. But beginning in 1405, these nations stopped the trade. They would no longer let the goods go through. And the people of Europe knew of no other way to get to Asia or India. They had not yet found their way around the southern point of Africa.

## Columbus tries to get help in carrying out his plans

Columbus was too poor to fit out even a single ship to undertake the voyage he had planned. In 1485, he asked the king of Portugal to furnish some money or vessels. But the king refused. A year later, Columbus went to Spain to see if he could get help there.

Columbus begging at the convent.

On the southern coast of Spain there is a small port named Palos.[6] Within sight of Palos, and also within sight of the ocean, there was a convent[7] called the Convent of Saint Mary.

One morning a tall, fine-looking man led a little boy by the hand and knocked at the door of the convent. The man begged for a piece of bread and a cup of water for the child. The man was Columbus. His wife had died and the boy was his son.

The guardian of the convent happened to notice Columbus standing at the door. He liked Columbus' appearance and decided to talk with him. Columbus told him about his dream. The guardian of the convent listened with great interest, then he gave Columbus a letter to a friend. He thought the friend might help Columbus present his plans before Ferdinand and Isabella,[8] the king and queen of Spain.

## Columbus gets help for his great voyage

Columbus left his son at the convent and set out on his journey. He was full of bright hopes. But Ferdinand and Isabella were unable to see him at that time. After waiting a long time, someone urged Columbus to speak with some learned men about his proposed voyage across the Atlantic.

After hearing what Columbus had to say, these men thought it would be foolish to spend money trying to reach the other side of the ocean. They were convinced Columbus had miscalculated the distance to China. They figured it would be too far. (As it turns out, they were correct. But they didn't know America was in the way.)

---

6  Palos (Pa'los); see Map 3, p. 9.
7  Convent: a house in which people live who devote themselves to a religious life.
8  Isabella (Iz-ah-bel'ah).

People who heard what Columbus, this captain from Lisbon, wanted to do began to think he had lost his reason. Boys in the streets laughed at him and called him crazy. Columbus waited seven years. Then he made up his mind to wait no longer. Just as he was about to leave Spain, Queen Isabella, who had always felt interested in the brave sailor, decided to help him. Two rich sea-captains who lived in Palos also decided to take part in the voyage. With the assistance that Columbus now got, he was able to fit out three small vessels. He went in the largest of the vessels—the only one that had an entire deck—as admiral, or commander, of the fleet.

## Columbus sails

Early on Friday morning, August 3, 1492, Columbus started from Palos in his attempt to cross the ocean that people then called the "Sea of Darkness." The name shows how little they knew of it, and how much they dreaded it.

We may be pretty sure that the guardian of the convent was one of those who watched the little fleet sail away. From the upper windows of the convent, he could plainly see the vessels as they left the harbor of Palos.

## What happened on the first part of the voyage

Columbus sailed first for the Canary Islands, because, he thought, from there it would be a straight line across to Japan and Asia. He was forced to stop at the Canaries[9] for more than three weeks. One of his vessels needed a new rudder. Another needed to alter its sails.

Eventually, all was ready, and he again set out on his voyage toward the west. When the sailors got so far out on the ocean

---

9   Canary Islands: See Map 3, p. 9.

that they could no longer see any of the islands, they were overcome with fear. They were convinced they would never be able to get back to Palos again. They were rough men, used to the sea, but now they bowed down their heads and cried like children. Columbus had hard work to quiet their fears and to encourage them to go forward with the voyage that they already wanted to give up.

Columbus refuses to turn back.

### What happened after they had been at sea many days

For more than 30 days, the three ships kept on their way toward the west. To the crew, every day seemed a year. From sunrise to sunset, they could see nothing but water and sky. At last, the men began to think they were sailing on an ocean that had no end. They whispered among themselves that Columbus had gone mad, and if they kept on with him in command they would all be lost.

Twice, indeed, there was a joyful cry of Land! Land!, but when they got nearer, they saw that what they had thought was land was nothing but banks of clouds. Then some of the sailors said, "Let's go to the admiral and tell him that we must turn back."

"What if he will not listen to us?" asked others.

"Then we will throw him overboard and say, when we reach Palos, that he fell into the sea and was drowned."

But when the crew went to Columbus and told him that they would go no further, he sternly ordered them to their work, declaring that, whatever might happen, he would not now give up the voyage.

## Signs of land

The very next day, the sailors saw signs of land that gave the most faint-hearted courage. The men had already noticed great flocks of land-birds flying toward the west. It was as if the birds were there to guide them. Then some of the men on one vessel saw a branch of a thorn-bush float by. It was plain that it had not long been broken off from the bush, and it was full of red berries.

But, then, one of the crew members on another vessel found something even better. He drew out of the water a carved walking-stick. Everyone could tell that such a stick must have been cut and carved by human hands. No one could doubt these two signs. The men now felt sure that they were approaching the shore and, more importantly, that there were people living in the country.

## Discovery of land

That evening, Columbus begged his crew to keep a sharp lookout, and he promised a velvet coat to whoever first saw land. Everyone was now excited and no man closed his eyes to sleep that night.

Columbus himself stood on a high part of his ship. He looked steadily toward the west. About ten o'clock he saw a moving light. It seemed like a torch carried in a man's hand.

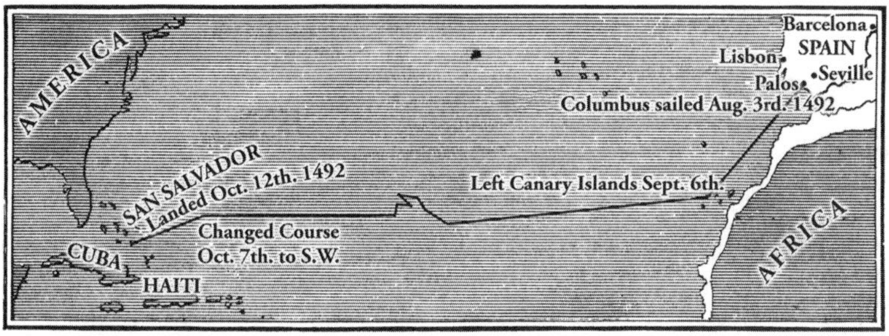

Map 3. The direction Columbus sailed on his great voyage across the ocean.

He called to a companion and asked him if he could see anything of the kind. Yes, he, too, plainly saw the moving light, but presently it disappeared.

Two hours after midnight, the lead vessel fired a cannon. It was the glad signal that this long-looked-for land was actually in sight. There it lay, directly ahead, about six miles distant.

Then Columbus gave the order to furl[10] sails. The three vessels came to a stop and waited for the dawn. When the sun rose on Friday, October 12, 1492, Columbus saw a beautiful island with many trees growing on it. It was his first sight of the New World, though he was convinced he was in India.

## Columbus lands on the island and names it; who lived on the island

Columbus was accompanied by the captains of the other two vessels and by their crews as he set out in a boat for the island. When the men landed, they all fell on their knees, kissed the ground for joy, and gave thanks to God. Columbus named the island San Salvador ("Holy Redeemer" or "Savior").

---

10 Furl: to roll up.

9

He also took possession of it for the king and queen of Spain. He claimed "right of discovery."[11]

Columbus found that the island was inhabited by a copper-colored people who spoke a language he couldn't understand. These people had never seen a ship or a white man before. They wore no clothes. Instead, they painted their bodies with bright colors. The Spaniards gave them presents of red caps and strings of glass beads. In return, the people gave the Spaniards skeins[12] of cotton yarn, tame parrots, and small ornaments of gold.

After staying a short time, Columbus set sail toward the south. He wanted to see if there was more land. And he hoped to find where these people got their gold.

## Columbus names the group of islands and their people

As Columbus sailed on, he saw many islands in every direction. He thought that they must be a part of the Indies which, of course, he had been seeking. Since he had reached them by coming west from Spain, he called them the West Indies. And to the darker-skinned people who lived there, he gave the name "Indians."

---

11 The "right of discovery" was, at the time Columbus landed in San Salvador, based on two bulls—or decrees—by the Pope. One was made in 1452, the other in 1455. Both bulls said much the same thing. In essence: "We grant you [Catholic kings] full permission to invade and rule any unbelievers and enemies of Christ wherever they may be found. We also grant you the right to turn these people into perpetual slaves." Once a king acquired the right to a certain land, the bulls then went on to say that any other kings—unless specifically licensed to do so—had no right "to sail to ... or to trade in [the] ports" of such subjugated lands.

12 Skein (skān): a length of thread or yarn wound in a loose long coil.

Landing of Columbus.

## Columbus discovers two very large islands, his vessel is wrecked, and he returns to Spain in another

Over the next six weeks, Columbus discovered the island of Cuba. At first he thought it must be Japan. But afterward, he decided it was not an island at all, but part of the main-land of Asia.

Next, he came to the island of Haiti, or San Domingo.[13] Here his ship was wrecked. He took the timber of the wreck and built a fort on the shore. Leaving about 40 of his crew in this fort, Columbus set sail for Palos in one of the two remaining vessels.

---

13 San Domingo: what we now know as the Dominican Republic. See Map 4, p. 13.

## Columbus arrives at Palos; joy of the people; how Ferdinand and Isabella received him

When Columbus' ship entered the harbor of Palos, the whole village went wild with excitement. More than seven months had gone by since he sailed away from that port. Since nothing had been heard from him, many supposed that the vessels and all on board were lost. Now that they saw their friends and neighbors coming back, all was joy. The bells of the churches rang a merry peal of welcome. The people thronged the streets, shouting to each other that Columbus, the great navigator, had crossed the "Sea of Darkness" and had returned safely.

At the time, the king and queen were in the city of Barcelona,[14] a long distance from Palos. Columbus now went there. He entered on horseback. He was accompanied by the proudest and richest noblemen of Spain. He brought with him six Indians from the West Indies. They were brightly painted and wore colorful feathers in their hair. Then a number of men followed. They carried rare birds, plants, and ornaments made of gold and silver. All of these things had been found in the New World. They were presents for the king and queen.

Ferdinand and Isabella received Columbus with great honor. When he had told them the story of his wonderful voyage, they sank on their knees and gave praise to God. All who were present followed their example.

## The last voyages of Columbus

Columbus made three more voyages across the Atlantic. He discovered more islands near the coast of America, and he

---

14 Barcelona (Bar-se-lo'na); See Map 3, p. 9.

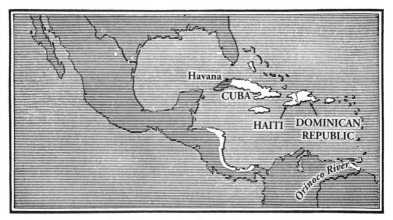

Map 4. The light parts of this map show how much of America Columbus discovered. The long island is Cuba; the large one to the right is San Domingo.

touched the coast of Central America and of South America, but that was all. He never set foot on any part of what is now the United States, and he always thought that the land he had reached was part of Asia. He had found a new world, but he did not know it. All that he knew was how to get to it and how to show others the way.

## Columbus in his old age

The last days of this great man were very sorrowful. The king was disappointed because Columbus brought back little gold to Spain. The Spanish governor of San Domingo hated Columbus; and when Columbus landed on that island during one of his voyages, the governor had him arrested and sent him back to Spain in chains. He was set free at once; but he could not forget the insult. He kept the chains hanging on the wall of his room, and asked to have them buried with him.

Columbus was now an old man. His health was broken; he was poor, in debt, and without a home. Once he wrote to the king and queen: "I have not a hair upon me that is not gray. My body is weak, and all that was left to me ... has been taken away and sold—even the coat I wore."

Not long after he had come back to Spain to stay, the queen died. Then Columbus felt that he had lost his best friend. He gave up hope and said, "I have done all that I could do. I leave the rest to God."

## His death and burial

Columbus died full of disappointment and sorrow. Perhaps it would not be too much to say that he died of a broken heart.

At first he was buried in Spain. Then his body was taken up and carried to San Domingo, where he had wished to be buried. Whether it rests there today, or whether it was carried to Havana[15] and deposited in the cathedral or great church of that city, no one can say for sure. But wherever the grave of the great sailor may be, his memory will live in every heart that can respect a brave man; for he was the first who dared to cross the "Sea of Darkness." And it was he who discovered for Europeans the land that we know as America.

## Summary

In 1492, Christopher Columbus set sail from Spain to find a direct way across the Atlantic to Asia and the Indies. He did not get to Asia. But, in many ways, he did better; he discovered America. Columbus died still thinking that the new lands he had found were part of Asia. But by his daring voyage, he first showed the people of Europe how to get to the New World.

---

15 Havana (Ha-van'ah): a city of Cuba. See Map 4, p. 13.

# Questions

When and where was Columbus born?

What did he do when he was fourteen?

What about his sea-fight?

What did he do in Lisbon?

How much of the world was then known?

How did Columbus think he could reach Asia and the Indies?

Why did he want to go there?

What did he try to do in Portugal?

Why did he go to Spain?

Where did he first go in Spain?

How did Columbus get help at last?

When did he sail?

What happened on the first part of the voyage?

What happened after that?

What were the signs of land that the men saw?

When did they actually see the land?

What did Columbus name the island where he first landed?

What did he find on it?

What happened when Columbus returned to Spain?

What about the last voyages of Columbus?

Did he ever land on any part of what is now the United States?

What happened in his old age?

Where was he buried?

Is he still buried there?

Why do people think of Columbus as a hero?

# John Cabot

Lived in England from 1472-1498

Map 5. Lisbon, Palos, Genoa and Venice.

## John Cabot discovers the *continent* of North America

Zuan Chabotto, or John Cabot, as most Americans know of him, was an Italian merchant from the city of Venice.[1] At the time Columbus set out on his first voyage across the Atlantic, Cabot (or Chabotto) was living in the port city of Bristol,[2] England.

When the news reached Bristol that Columbus had discovered the West Indies, Cabot begged Henry VII, king of England, to let him see if he could find a shorter way to the Indies than that of Columbus. The king gave his consent, and in the spring of 1497, Cabot sailed from Bristol with his son and a crew of about twenty on a small ship named the *Matthew* of Bristol. They headed northwest. They hoped that, by going in that direction, they would get to those parts of Asia and the Spice

Map 6. "Land First Seen" and Nova Scotia.

---

1 Venice, Italy: See Map 5, p. 16.
2 Bristol, England: See Map 12, p. 50.

16

Islands that were known to Europe but that Columbus had failed to reach.

Early one bright morning toward the end of June 1497, they saw land in the west. It was probably Cape Breton[3] Island, a part of Nova Scotia.[4] John Cabot named it "The Land First Seen."

Up to this time, Columbus had discovered nothing but the West India Islands, but John Cabot now saw the continent of North America. No one from Western Europe had ever seen it before.[5] There it lay, a great, lonely land, shaggy with forests, with not a house or a human being in sight.

Cabot taking possession for England.

## John Cabot takes possession of the country for the king of England

Cabot went on shore with his son and some of his crew. They went no more than a hundred yards inland, but

---

3   Breton (Bret'un).

4   Nova Scotia (No'vuh Sko'shuh). See Map 6, p. 16.

5   A man named Erik Thorvaldsson—"Erik the Red"—led an expedition of men to North America about five hundred years before Cabot did, Erik's men came from Scandinavia (in the North of Europe, where Norway, Sweden and Denmark are). They were known as Vikings. Other Europeans considered them pirates and murderers. Erik's men came to what we now know as Greenland. Sadly, nothing came of the Vikings' discovery. When Cabot sailed, no one seems to have known anything about what the Vikings had done so long before.

they found some nets, a wooden tool, the remains of a fire, and a human trail. They found no people.

They set up a large cross, planted two flag-poles, and hoisted the English flag on one and the flag of Cabot's home city, Venice, on the other. Then they took possession of the land for Henry VII. It was in this way that the English came to consider that the eastern coast of North America was their property, although they didn't begin to make settlements there until nearly a hundred years later.

## John Cabot returns to Bristol

John Cabot and his crew sailed about the Gulf of St. Lawrence[6] but found no passage to Asia. So the voyagers returned to England.

Even though he failed to discover a way to Asia, the king was so pleased with Cabot's discovery that he gave him a reward of £10[7] — equivalent to about two years' pay for an ordinary laborer or craftsman at the time. When the captain, richly dressed in silk, appeared in the street, the people of Bristol would "run after him like mad" and hurrah for the "Great Admiral," as they called him.

## What Cabot carried back to England from America

Cabot and his crew carried back to England some Indian traps for catching game and, perhaps, some wild turkeys. The English had never seen turkeys before, but they were glad to make their acquaintance. The crew also carried the rib of a whale they had found on the beach in Nova Scotia.

---

6   Gulf of St. Lawrence: See Map 6, p. 16.
7   £10: Ten pounds British sterling; a sum of money.

There is a famous old church near where the Cabots are believed to have lived. The church of St. Mary Redcliffe was built long before the discovery of America, and Queen Elizabeth said that it was the most beautiful building of its kind in all England. In that church hangs the rib of a whale. People say it is the one that John Cabot brought home with him. It reminds all who see it of that voyage in 1497 by which England gained possession of a very large part of the continent of North America.

## How the New World came to be called America

But not many years after this the New World received the name by which we now call it. An Italian navigator whose first name was Amerigo[8] made a voyage to it after it had been discovered by Columbus and the Cabots. He wrote an account of what he saw, and as this was the first printed description of the continent, it was named from him, AMERICA.

Map 7. The light parts of this map show how much of the continent of North America was discovered by the Cabots.

## Summary

John Cabot, an Italian merchant from Venice, convinced the king of England to sponsor a voyage of discovery to

---

8  Amerigo (Ah-meh-ree'go): his full name was Amerigo Vespucci (Veh-spoo'chee), or, as he wrote it in Latin, Americus Vespucius.

the west. In 1497, Cabot sailed from Bristol, England, and discovered the mainland–or continent–of North America, and took possession of it for England.

An Italian whose first name was Amerigo visited the New World afterward and wrote the first account of the mainland that came into print. It was for this reason that the whole continent was named after him: AMERICA.

## Questions

Who was John Cabot?

What did he try to do?

Who sailed with him?

What land did they see?

Had Columbus ever seen it?

What did Cabot do when he went on shore?

What happened when he returned to Bristol?

What did Cabot carry back to England?

How did the New World come to be called America?

# Ponce de Leon,[1] Balboa,[2] and de Soto[3]

Period of Discovery, 1513-1542

---

## The magic fountain; Ponce de Leon discovers Florida; Balboa discovers the Pacific Ocean

The Indians on the West India Islands believed that there was a wonderful fountain in a land to the west of them. They said that if an old man could bathe in its waters, they would make him a boy again. Ponce de Leon, a Spanish soldier who was getting gray and wrinkled, set out to find this magic fountain. After all, he thought, it was more fun to be a boy than to grow old.

De Leon did not find the fountain, and so his hair grew grayer than ever and his wrinkles grew deeper. But in 1513 he discovered a land bright with flowers. He named it Florida.[4] He took possession of it for Spain.

The same year, another Spaniard, named Balboa, set out to explore the Isthmus[5] of Panama. One day he climbed to the top of a very high hill, and saw a vast ocean—the greatest of all the oceans of the globe. We call it the Pacific.

---

1   Ponce de Leon (Pon'thay day Lay-own') or, in English, Pons de Lay-own'.
2   Balboa (Bal-bo'uh).
3   de Soto (da So'to).
4   Florida: this word means flowery; the Spaniards gave it this name because they discovered the country on Easter Sunday, which they call Flowery Easter.
5   Isthmus: a narrow strip of land with sea on either side, that forms a link between two larger areas of land.

## De Soto discovers the Mississippi

Long after Balboa and Ponce de Leon were dead, a Spaniard named de Soto landed in Florida and marched through the country. He was looking for gold mines.

De Soto's first view of the Mississippi River.

In the course of his long and weary wanderings, he came to a river more than a mile across. The Indians told him it was the Mississippi, or the Great River. De Soto had found the largest river in North America. He had also found his own grave, for he died shortly after, and was secretly buried at midnight in its muddy waters.

## The Spaniards build St. Augustine;[6] the United States buys Florida in 1819

More than twenty years after the burial of de Soto, a Spanish soldier named Menendez[7] went to Florida and built a fort on the eastern coast. It was 1565. The fort became the center of a settlement named St. Augustine. It is the oldest city built by Europeans, not only in what is now the United States, but in all of North America.

---

6   St. Augustine (Saint Aw'gus-teen'). See Map 7, p. 19.
7   Menendez (Muh-nen'deth or Muh-nen'dez).

Old Spanish gateway at St. Augustine.
Called the "City Gate."

In 1819, or more than two hundred and fifty years after St. Augustine was founded, Spain sold Florida to the United States.

## Summary

Ponce de Leon discovered Florida; another Spaniard, named Balboa, discovered the Pacific; still another, named de Soto, discovered the Mississippi. In 1565 the Spaniards began to build St. Augustine in Florida. It is the oldest city built by Europeans in the United States and in all of North America.

## Questions

The West India Indians talked about a magic fountain. What was it supposed to do?

What did Ponce de Leon do?

What did Balboa do?

And de Soto—what did he do?

What did Menendez do in Florida?

What is special about St. Augustine?

# Sir Walter Raleigh[1]

### 1552-1618

## Walter Raleigh sends two ships to America; how the Indians received the Englishmen

Although John Cabot discovered the continent of North America in 1497 and took possession of the land for England, the English themselves did not try to settle there until nearly a hundred years later.

Sir Walter Raleigh.

Map 8. Roanoke Island.

It was in 1584 that a young man named Walter Raleigh, a great favorite of Queen Elizabeth, sent two ships to America. The captains of these vessels landed on Roanoke[2] Island, on the coast of what is now the State of North Carolina. They found the island covered with tall red cedars and with vines thick with clusters of wild grapes. The Indians called this place the "Good Land." They were pleased to see the

---

1  Raleigh (Raw'lee).
2  Roanoke (Ro-uh-noke'): See Map 8, p. 24.

Englishmen, and they invited them to a great feast of roast turkey, venison,[3] melons, and nuts.

## Queen Elizabeth names the country Virginia; first settlers; what they sent Walter Raleigh

When the two captains returned to England, Queen Elizabeth was delighted with what she heard of the "Good Land." Named the "Virgin Queen" because she had never married, she named the new land Virginia, in honor of herself. She also gave Raleigh a title of honor. From that time he was no longer called plain Walter Raleigh or Mr. Raleigh, but Sir Walter Raleigh.

Sir Walter now, in 1585, shipped over emigrants[4] to settle in Virginia. They sent back to him as a present two famous American plants. One was called Tobacco, the other the Potato. The queen had given Sir Walter a fine estate in Ireland, and he set out both of these plants in his garden. The tobacco plant did not grow very well there, but the potato did; and after a time thousands of farmers began to raise that vegetable, not only in Ireland, but in England too. As far back, then, as that time, the late 1500s, America began to feed the people of the Old World.

The first European pipe of tobacco.

Raleigh's servant thought his master was on fire.

---

3   Venison (ven'i-sun): deer meat.
4   Emigrants: people who leave one country to settle in another.

## The Virginia settlement destroyed

Sir Walter spent immense sums of money on his Roanoke Island settlement in Virginia, but it did not succeed. One of the settler families, the Dares, had a daughter born there. They named her Virginia. Virginia Dare was the first English child born in America. But the little girl, with her father, mother, and all the rest of the settlers, disappeared. It is supposed that they were either killed by the Indians or that they wandered away and starved to death; but all that we really know is that not one of them was ever seen again.

## Last days of Sir Walter Raleigh

After Queen Elizabeth died, King James I became ruler of England. He accused Sir Walter of trying to take away his crown so as to make someone else ruler over the country. Sir Walter was sent to prison and kept there for many years. At last King James released him in order to send him to South America to get gold. When Sir Walter returned to London without any gold, the greedy king accused him of having disobeyed him because he had fought with some Spaniards. Raleigh was condemned to death and beheaded.

But Sir Walter's attempt to settle Virginia led other Englishmen to try. Before he died, they built a town, called Jamestown, on the coast. We shall presently read the history of that town. The English held Virginia from that time until it became part of the United States.

## Summary

Sir Walter Raleigh sent over men from England to explore the coast of America. Queen Elizabeth named the country they visited Virginia. Raleigh then shipped emigrants over to make a settlement. These emigrants sent him two American plants, Tobacco and the Potato; and in that way the people of Great Britain and Ireland came to like both. Sir Walter's settlement failed, but his example led other Englishmen to try to make another settlement. Before he was beheaded, they succeeded.

## Questions

What did Walter Raleigh do?

How did the Indians greet the Englishmen when they first arrived?

What name did Queen Elizabeth give to the country?

What did she do for Walter Raleigh?

What did Sir Walter then do?

What American plants did the emigrants send him?

What did he do with those plants?

What happened to the Virginia settlement?

What happened to Sir Walter Raleigh when Queen Elizabeth died?

Did Sir Walter's attempt to settle Virginia do any good?

# Captain John Smith

1579-1631

Captain John Smith.

### New and successful attempt to make a settlement in Virginia; Captain John Smith

Captain John Smith was one of the leaders in the new expedition sent to make a settlement in Virginia. Smith began life as a clerk in England. He didn't enjoy his work, so he ran away and became a soldier. After many strange adventures, he was captured by the Turks[1] and sold as a slave. His master riveted a heavy iron collar around his neck and set him to thrashing grain with a big wooden bat. One day, Smith's master rode up and struck him with his riding-whip. This was more than Smith could bear. He rushed at his master and used the man's own bat against him. Smith then mounted the dead man's horse and escaped. After a time, he got back to England. But as England seemed a little dull to Captain Smith, he resolved to join some emigrants who were going to Virginia.

---

1 Turks: people from Turkey. At the time, the Turkish empire ruled much of the eastern Mediterranean.

**What happened to Captain Smith on the voyage; the landing at Jamestown; what the settlers wanted to do; Smith's plan**

On the way to America, Smith was accused of plotting to murder the chief men among the settlers so that he might make himself "King of Virginia." The accusation was false, but he was put in irons and kept a prisoner for the rest of the voyage.

In April of 1607, the emigrants reached Chesapeake Bay, and sailed up a river that they named the James, in honor of King James of England. When they landed, they named their new settlement Jamestown for the same reason. Here they built a log fort and placed three or four small cannons on its walls.

Most of the men who settled Jamestown came hoping to find mines of gold, or else a way through to the Pacific Ocean and to the Indies, which they thought could not be very far away. But Captain Smith wanted to help his countrymen make homes for themselves and their children.

**Smith's trial and what came of it; how the settlers lived; the first English church; sickness; attempted desertion**

Map 9. The Jamestown Colony.

As soon as Captain Smith landed, he demanded to be tried by a jury[2] of twelve men. The trial took place. It was the first English court and the first English jury that ever sat in America. The captain proved his

---

2   Jury: a group of people selected according to law to try a case in a court of law. In criminal cases, they declare the person accused to be either guilty or not guilty.

innocence and was set free. His chief accuser was condemned to pay him a large sum of money for damages. Smith generously gave this money to help the settlement.

Since the weather was warm, the emigrants did not begin building log cabins at once. Instead, they slept on the ground, sheltered by boughs of trees. They used an old tent as a church building. They were all members of the Church of England, or the Episcopal Church, and that tent was the first place of worship we know of that was opened by Englishmen in America.

When the hot weather came, many fell sick. Soon the whole settlement was like a hospital. One hundred and four men had landed in Jamestown. By September, more than 60 of them had died. Captain Smith, though not well himself, did everything he could for those who needed his help.

When the sickness was over, some of the settlers were so unhappy that they determined to seize the only vessel there was at Jamestown and go back to England. Captain Smith turned the cannon of the fort against them. The deserters saw that if they tried to leave the harbor, he would knock their ship to pieces, so they came back. One of the leaders of these men was tried and shot; the other was sent to England in disgrace.

## The Indians of Virginia

When the Indians of the New World first met the Europeans, they were very friendly to them. But this didn't last long, because most of the European settlers treated the Indians very badly. In fact, the Spaniards made slaves of the Indians they met, and whipped many of them to death. These were the Indians of the south. Some of the northern tribes were stronger and proved a match for the Spaniards in cruelty.

The Indians in the northeastern part of North America did not build cities, but lived in small villages. These villages were made of huts that were covered with the bark of trees. These huts were called wigwams.

The women did nearly all the work. It was their job to build the wigwams and to care for the corn and tobacco crops. The men hunted and made war.

Instead of guns, the Indians had bows and arrows. But they could bring down a deer or squirrel quite as well as any Englishman could with a musket.[3]

The Indians had no iron, but made hatchets and knives out of sharp, flat stones. They never built roads, because they had no wagons. And in the east they did not use horses. But they could find their way with ease through the thickest forests. When Indians came to a river, they swam across it, so they had no need of bridges. For boats, they made canoes of birch bark. These canoes, to the English, seemed as light as paper, yet they were very strong and handsome. The poet Henry Wadsworth Longfellow described these canoes in his famous poem *Hiawatha*. He said they

> ... floated on the river
> Like a yellow leaf in autumn,
> Like a yellow water-lily.

---

3    Musket: a long-barreled gun. In the mid-1800s, rifles came to replace muskets. The difference between the two guns: the inside of a musket's barrel (what is called the "bore") is smooth; rifles have spiral grooves ("rifles") cut in their bores. The grooves make a rifle's bullets spin, so they travel accurately to their target. Musket bullets, having no spin, tumble and fly unpredictably, so one can never be sure where the bullet will go.

The Indians could go hundreds of miles in these canoes quickly and silently. So every river and stream became a roadway.

## Captain Smith goes in search of the Pacific; he is captured by Indians

After that first long, hot summer, some of the surviving settlers wanted to explore the country and see if they could find a short way through to the Pacific Ocean. Captain Smith led the expedition.

Captain John Smith before Powhatan.

According to Smith, some Indians attacked the party, killed three of the men, and took him prisoner. To amuse the Indians, he showed them his pocket compass. When his captors saw that the needle always pointed toward the north, they were greatly astonished, and, instead of killing him, they decided to take him to their chief. The chief was named Powhatan.[4] He was a tall, grim-looking old man.

---

4   Powhatan (Pow-ha-tun'). This was his name, we are told, according to what the Indians first told the English settlers. And this has become the standard name by which he is known. However, further research shows that Powhatan was the name of the place where he was born. The name by which his people referred to him was Wahunsunacock (Wa-hun-sun'-uh-cock). At the time the English arrived, he was the leader of a confederacy of about 30 tribes and between 10,000 to 15,000 people.

## Smith's life is saved by Pocahontas;[5] her marriage to John Rolfe

According to a record that Smith wrote 17 years after the event, he was brought into the chief's wigwam, given a great feast, and then, suddenly, forced to lay his head on a large, flat stone. A tall Indian with a big club got up, apparently ready to execute him. Then, said Smith, just as Powhatan was about to kill him, Powhatan's daughter, Pocahontas, a girl of twelve or thirteen, ran up. She put her arms around Smith's head, laid her own head on his, and, thus, saved Smith's life (since, in order to kill Smith, the executioner would first have to kill Pocahontas).

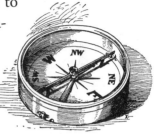

Pocket compass.

Instead of being angry with his daughter, Powhatan promised Pocahontas that he would spare Smith's life ... at which point the captain knew his head was safe. Powhatan released his prisoner and soon sent him back to Jamestown. Meanwhile, Pocahontas and a number of other Indians, brought the English settlers presents of corn and venison.[6]

Some years after this, Pocahontas married John Rolfe, an Englishman who had come to Virginia. They went to London, and Pocahontas died not far from that city. She

---

5  Pocahontas (Po-kuh-hon'tus).

6  It is quite possible—indeed, probable—that Smith perceived most of the events he described exactly as he portrayed them. However, assuming he gave the details as accurately as possible, were the circumstances *really* as Smith *perceived* them? A large number of modern historians believe the entire event may have been intended as a gesture of peace on the part of Powhatan. The series of events with Pocahontas, especially, these scholars say, was an adoption ritual by which Powhatan sought to establish his sovereignty over Smith and the English settlers. In essence, he was saying, "It is only by my kindness that I let you live. If you maintain faithfulness to me as your sovereign lord, I will protect you." The gifts of corn and venison were symbols of Powhatan's good faith.

left a son. From that son came some noted Virginians. One of them was John Randolph. He was a famous man in his day, and he always spoke with pride of the Indian princess, as he called her.

## Captain Smith is made governor of Jamestown; the gold-diggers; "Corn, or your life."

More than 200 additional emigrants came over from England in 1608, and in September of that year, just before the final ship arrived (which was the first ship to bring English women), Captain Smith was elected president of the Jamestown colony[7] and head of the council.

Shortly after, some of the emigrants found some glittering earth which they thought was gold. Soon nearly every one of them could be seen hard at work digging for gold. Smith told them they were wasting their time; but they insisted on loading a ship with the stuff and sending it to London. That was the last they heard of it.

The truth was, these men had wasted their time. They had been digging iron pyrite—fool's gold—when they could have been far better employed hoeing their gardens.

Meanwhile, hundreds of additional emigrants joined the starving colonists in Jamestown. And the new arrivals brought little food and had no desire to work.

The Indians had supplied the colonists with gifts of corn and meat during their first winter in the new land. But Powhatan became alarmed as he saw the colonists' numbers keep increasing. He also noticed their unwillingness to provide for themselves. And he became increasingly upset by the

7   Colony: a company of settlers who came to America from England, and who were subject to the king of England.

frequent incidents of English colonists' outright theft of food and destruction of Indian villages when the inhabitants refused to grant the English whatever they demanded. Why should his people continue to support these Englishmen who could not be bothered to meet their own needs?

When English settlers came begging for food, he began refusing and, instead, asked when they would return home.

In January of 1609, Captain Smith decided to forgo words. He set off with a party of 40 men to acquire food from the Indians by force. Powhatan greeted them in a friendly manner, but that night, two informers (one being Pocahontas) warned Smith that Powhatan intended to kill him and his men. The next day, while surrounded by hundreds of Indian warriors, Smith seized Powhatan's brother by the hair, pressed the muzzle of a pistol against his heart, and gave him the ultimatum,—"Corn, or your life!"

"Corn, or your life!"

Smith got the corn. But the stage was set for further violence.

## "He who will not work shall not eat."

Captain Smith now realized the settlers' situation was grave and he could not rely on the Indians to supply all the settlers' needs. He set part of the men to planting corn, so that they might raise what they needed. The rest of the settlers he took with him into the woods to chop down trees and saw them into boards to send to England. Many tried to escape from this labor; but Smith said, "Men who are able to dig for gold are able to chop." Then he made this rule: "He who will not work shall not eat." Rather than lose his dinner, the laziest man now took his axe and set off for the woods.

## Captain Smith's cold-water cure

Though the choppers worked, they grumbled. They liked to see the chips fly and to hear the great trees "thunder as they fell," but the axe-handles raised blisters on their fingers. These blisters made the men swear, so that often one would hear an oath for every stroke of the axe. Smith said the swearing must be stopped. He had each man's oaths set down in a book. When the day's work was done, every offender was called up; his oaths were counted; then he was told to hold up his right hand, and a can of cold water was poured down his sleeve for each oath. This new style of water cure did wonders. In a short time, not an oath was heard. It was just chop, chop, chop. And the madder the men got, the more the chips would fly.

## Captain Smith meets with an accident and goes back to England; his return to America; his death

Captain Smith had been governor for just about a year when he met with a terrible accident. He was out in his canoe when a bag of gunpowder he had with him exploded. He was so badly hurt that he had to go back to England to get proper treatment for his wounds. It was October of 1609.

Once he recovered, Smith begged the Virginia Company officials to permit him to return to Jamestown, but the company officials refused. Eventually, in 1614, he returned to America in order to explore the coast north of Virginia. He gave these territories the name New England. With the idea that he would start a colony in the new territory, he set sail for New England once more in 1615. On his way, however, he was captured by French pirates. He escaped and went back to England from which he never left again. He died in London, and was buried in a famous old church in that city.[8]

## What Captain Smith did for Virginia

Captain John Smith was in Virginia less than three years, yet in that short time he did a great deal. First, he saved the settlers from starving, by making the Indians sell them corn. Next, by his courage, he saved them from the attacks of the Indians. Lastly, he taught them how to work.

Had it not been for him, it seems, the people of Jamestown would probably have lost all heart and gone back to England.

He insisted on their staying, and so, through him, the English got their first real foothold in America. But this was not all; he wrote two books on Virginia. He described the soil, the trees, the animals, and the Indians. He also made some excellent maps of Virginia and of New England. These books and maps taught the English people many things about America, and helped those who wished to emigrate to do so. For these reasons Captain Smith has rightfully been called the "Father of Virginia."

A settler's log cabin.

---

8   The church of St. Sepulchre: it is not very far from St. Paul's Cathedral.

## African slaves sent to Virginia; tobacco

About ten years after Captain Smith left Jamestown, the commander of a Dutch ship brought a number of African captives to Virginia (1619) and sold them to the settlers as slaves. That was the beginning of slavery in North America. Later, when other English settlements had been made, they bought slaves, too, and so, after a time, every settlement north as well as south of Virginia owned more or fewer black slaves. The European settlers of Virginia employed most of their slaves in raising tobacco. They sold their tobacco in England, and, as it generally brought a good price, many of the planters[9] became quite rich.

## Bacon's war against Governor Berkeley;[10] Jamestown burned

Long after Captain Smith was in his grave, Sir William Berkeley was made governor of Virginia by the king of England. He treated the people very badly. At last, a young planter named Bacon raised a small army and marched against the governor, who was in Jamestown. The governor, finding that he had few friends to fight for him, made haste to get out of the place. Bacon then entered it with his men; but as he knew that, if necessary, the king would send soldiers from England to aid the governor in getting it back, he set fire to the place and burned it to the ground. It was never built up again, and so only a crumbling church-tower and a few gravestones can now be seen where Jamestown once stood. Those ruins mark the first English town settled in America.

---

9  Planter: a person who owns a plantation or large farm. Such a plantation or farm is cultivated by laborers living on it. Until the late 1800s, almost all such laborers were African slaves.
10  Berkeley (Ber'kli).

## What happened later in Virginia; the Revolution; Washington; four presidents

Though Jamestown was destroyed, Virginia kept growing in strength and wealth. What was better still for the European immigrants, the larger North American territory grew in the number of leaders of European extraction. The king of England continued to rule America until, in 1776, the people of Virginia demanded that independence should be declared. The great war of the Revolution overthrew the king's power and made the English colonies free of British oversight. The military leader of that war was a Virginia planter named George Washington.

After the American colonies had gained victory, and peace was made, the newly-independent states chose a president to oversee their new federal government. Four out of six of the Union's first presidents, beginning with Washington, came from Virginia. For this reason that state has sometimes been called the "Mother of Presidents."

## Summary

In 1607 Captain John Smith, with others, made the first lasting settlement built up by Englishmen in America. Through Captain Smith's energy and courage, Jamestown, Virginia, took firm root. Virginia was the first colony to demand the independence of America, and Washington, who was a Virginian, led the war of the Revolution by which that independence was gained.

## Questions

What can you tell about Captain John Smith before he went to Virginia?

What happened to him on his way to Virginia?

What is said about the landing of the settlers in Virginia?

What did they want to do?

What did Captain Smith want to do?

What about Captain Smith's trial?

What happened to the settlers?

What did some of them try to do?

Who stopped them?

Tell what you can about the Indians.

What kind of houses did they live in?

Did they have guns?

Did they have iron hatchets and knives?

Did they have horses and wagons?

What kind of boats did they have?

What happened to Captain Smith when he went in search of the Pacific?

What did Pocahontas do?

What happened to her after this incident with Smith?

What about the gold-diggers: what happened to them?

How did Captain Smith get corn?

What do you think: were his actions right? Why or why not?

What did he make the settlers do?

What was Captain Smith's "cold-water cure" about?

Why did Captain Smith go back to England?

What did Captain Smith do for Virginia?

What about his books and maps?

What did you learn about black/African slaves from this chapter?

What about tobacco?

What about Governor Berkeley and Mr. Bacon?

What happened to Jamestown?

What did the war of the Revolution do?

Who was its great military leader?

Why is Virginia sometimes called the "Mother of Presidents"?

# Captain Henry Hudson

Voyages from 1607 to 1611

---

## Captain Hudson tries to find a northwest passage to China and the Indies

When Captain John Smith sailed for Virginia, he left a friend, Henry Hudson, back in London. Hudson was famous as one of the best sea-captains in England.

While Smith was in Jamestown, a company of London merchants sent Captain Hudson to try to discover a passage to China and the Indies. When he left England, he sailed to the northwest, hoping that he could find a way open to the Pacific across the North Pole or not far below it.

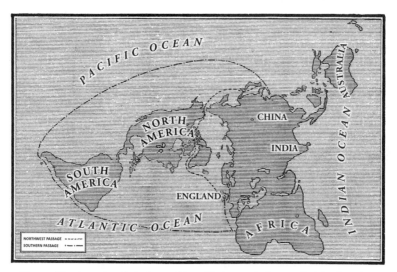

Map 10. The passage by which Captain Henry Hudson might have reached Asia by sailing northwest from England as compared to how vessels actually reached Asia by sailing down to the Canary Islands and then around the tip of South America. Distances are distorted. Please consult a globe for more accurate distance comparisons.

If he found such a passage, he knew that it would be much shorter than a voyage around the globe further south; because, as any one can see, it is not nearly so far round the top of an apple, near the stem, as it is round the middle.

Hudson could not find the passage he was looking for; but he saw mountains of ice, and he went nearer to the North Pole than any one had ever been before.

## The Dutch hire Captain Hudson; he sails for America

A company of Dutch merchants from the province of Holland in the Netherlands heard of Hudson's voyage. They hired the brave sailor to see if he could find a passage to Asia by sailing to the north and east.

Hudson set out from the port of Amsterdam[1] in 1609 in a vessel named the *Half Moon*. After he had gone quite a long distance, the sailors got so tired of seeing nothing but fog and ice that they refused to go any further.

Then Captain Hudson turned his ship about and sailed for the coast of North America. He did that because his friend, Captain Smith of Virginia, had sent him a letter, with a map, that made him think he could find such a passage north of Chesapeake Bay.

## Captain Hudson reaches America and finds the "Great River"

Hudson got to Chesapeake Bay, but the weather was so stormy that he thought it would not be safe to enter it. Therefore, he sailed northward along the coast. In September of 1609, he entered a beautiful bay at the entrance to a noble river. At that point the stream is more than a mile wide,

---

1   Amsterdam, Holland: See Map 12, p. 50.

and he called it the "Great River." On the eastern side of it, not far from its mouth, there is a long narrow island. The Indians of that day called it Manhattan Island.

## The tides in the "Great River"; Captain Hudson begins to sail up the stream

One of the remarkable things about the river that Hudson discovered is that it has hardly any current, and the tide from the ocean moves up for more than 150 miles. If no fresh water ran in from the hills, the sea would still fill the channel for a long distance. And so it makes a kind of salt-water river out of it. Hudson noticed how salty it was, and that, perhaps, made him think he had found a passage that would lead him from the Atlantic to the Pacific. He was delighted with all he saw, and said, "This is as beautiful a land as one can tread upon." Soon he began to sail up the stream, wondering what he would see and whether he might come out on an ocean that would take him to Asia.

## Hudson's voyage on the "Great River"; his feast with the Indians

At first Hudson drifted along, carried by the tide, under the shadow of a great natural wall of rock. That wall—what we

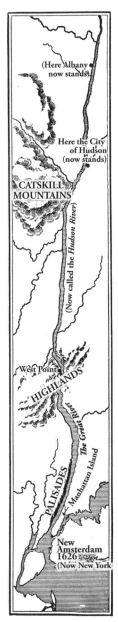

Map 11. Hudson's Great River.

now call the Palisades[2]—is from 400 to 600 feet high. It extends for nearly 20 miles along the western shore of the river.

Captain Hudson on the Great River.

Then, some distance further up, Captain Hudson came to a place where the river breaks through great forest-covered hills, called the Highlands. At the end of the fifth day, he came to a point on the eastern bank above the Highlands, where the city of Hudson, New York now stands. Here, an old Indian chief invited him to come ashore. Hudson had found the Indians, as he says, "very loving," so he thought he would accept the invitation. The Indians made a great feast for the captain. They gave him not only roast pigeons, but also a roast dog, which they cooked specially for him. They wanted him to have the very best.

These Indians had never seen a white man before. They thought that the English captain, in his bright scarlet coat trimmed with gold lace, might have come down from the sky to visit them. What puzzled them, however, was that he had such a pale face instead of a dark one like themselves.

At the end of the feast, Hudson rose to go, but the Indians begged him to stay all night. Then one of them got up, gathered all the arrows, broke them to pieces, and threw them

---

2   Palisades: this name is given to the wall of rock on the Hudson, because, when seen nearby, it somewhat resembles a palisade—a high fence made of stakes or posts set close together, upright in the ground.

into the fire, in order to show the captain that he need not be afraid to stay with them.

## Captain Hudson reaches the end of his voyage and turns back; trouble with the Indians

Captain Hudson made up his mind that he must now go on with his voyage. He went back to his ship and kept on up the river until he had reached a point about 150 miles from its mouth. This is where the city of Albany, New York, now stands. He found that the water was growing shallow, and he feared that if the *Half Moon* went further she would run aground. It was clear to him, too, that wherever the river might lead, he was not likely to find it a short road to China.

On the way downstream, an Indian, who had come out in a canoe, managed to steal something from the ship. One of the crew chanced to see the Indian as he was slipping off the boat and, picking up a gun, the crewman fired and killed the man. After that, Hudson's men had several fights with Indians.

## Hudson returns to Europe; the "Great River" is called by his name; his death

Early in October, the captain set sail for Europe. Ever since that time, the beautiful river that he explored has been called the Hudson in his honor.

The next year, Captain Hudson made another voyage, and entered that immense bay in the northern part of America that we now know as Hudson Bay in northeast Canada. There he got into trouble with his men. Some of them seized him and set him adrift with a few others in an open boat.

Nothing more was ever heard of the brave English sailor. The bay that bears his name is probably his grave.

## The Dutch take possession of the land on the Hudson and call it New Netherland; how New Netherland became New York

As soon as the Dutch merchants received the news that Captain Hudson had found a country where the people had rich furs to sell, they sent out representatives to trade with them. When these Dutch merchants took possession of the land on the Hudson (1614), they gave it the name New Netherland,[3] for the same reason that the English called one part of their possessions in North America New England. In the course of a few years, the Dutch built a fort (1615) and some log cabins on the lower end of Manhattan Island. After a time they named this little settlement New Amsterdam, in remembrance of the port of Amsterdam in Holland from which Hudson had sailed.

After the Dutch had held the country of New Netherland about 50 years, the English seized it (1664). They changed its name to New York, in honor of the Duke of York, who was brother to the English king. The English also changed the name of New Amsterdam to that of New York City.

## The New York "Sons of Liberty" in the Revolution; what Henry Hudson would say of the city now

More than a hundred years after the English took over, the young men of New York City, the "Sons of Liberty" as they called themselves, made ready with the "Sons of Liberty" in other English colonies to do their full part. They fought

---

3   New Netherland: this is often incorrectly printed New Netherlands.

under the lead of General Washington in the great war of the American Revolution. That was the war by which the European American colonists gained their freedom from the rule of the king of England, and became the United States of America.

The silent harbor where Henry Hudson saw a few Indian canoes is now one of the busiest seaports in the world. The great Statue of Liberty stands at its entrance. To it, a fleet of ships is constantly coming from all parts of the globe. From it, another fleet is constantly going. One can imagine: If Captain Hudson were to see the river that bears his name, and Manhattan Island now covered with miles of buildings that make it part of the largest and wealthiest city in America today, he would say: "I need not look any further for the riches of China and the Indies, for I have found them here."

## Summary

In 1609 Henry Hudson, an English sea-captain, then in the employ of the Dutch, discovered the river now called by his name. The Dutch took possession of the country on the river, named it New Netherland, and built a small settlement on Manhattan Island. Many years later, the English seized the country and named it New York. The settlement on Manhattan Island then became New York City; it is now the largest and wealthiest city in the United States.

## Questions

Who was Henry Hudson?

What did he try to find?

What did some Dutch merchants hire him to do?

Where did he go?

What did he call the river he discovered?

What can you tell about that river?

What happened on Hudson's voyage up the river?

Hudson and his crew encountered some Indians on their way up the river. Describe their experiences with the Indians.

Why did Hudson turn back when he reached the place on the river that is now Albany, New York?

What did Hudson do when he turned back?

What is the river he discovered now called?

What happened to Captain Hudson the next year?

What did the Dutch who had hired Hudson do when they heard about the land he had discovered?

What did they name the country? Why?

What did they build on Manhattan Island?

Who seized New Netherland from the Dutch?

What name did they give it?

Who were the "Sons of Liberty" and what did they do?

What did the author think Hudson would say if he could see New York City now?

Copyright by Charles T. Root.

Liberty enlightening the world.

A stature in the harbor of New York City, given to the American people
by the people of France.

# Captain Myles Standish
1584-1656

## The English Pilgrims in Holland; why they left England

Map 12. The English and Dutch homelands of the Pilgrims.

When the news of Henry Hudson's discovery of the Hudson River reached Holland, many Englishmen were living in the Dutch city of Leyden.[1] These people were mostly farmers who had fled from Scrooby[2] and neighboring villages in the northeast of England. They called themselves Pilgrims, because they were wanderers from their old homes.

The Pilgrims left England because King James would not let them hold their religious meetings in peace. He thought, as all kings in Europe did at that time, that everybody in his country should believe the same things, belong to the same church, and worship God in the same way that he did. King James was afraid that if people were allowed to believe whatever they wanted and went to whatever church they thought best, it would lead to disputes and quarrels. And that would break his kingdom into pieces.

---

1 Leyden (Li'den).
2 Scrooby (Skroo'bee).

Quite a number of Englishmen, seeing that they could not have religious liberty at home, escaped with their wives and children to Holland. In Holland, the Dutch were willing to let people worship however they wanted. These, then, were the Pilgrims.[3]

## Why the Pilgrims wished to leave Holland and go to America

The Pilgrims had gone to the Netherlands, but they were not content there. They saw that if they stayed in that country, their children would grow up to be more Dutch than English. They saw, too, that they could not hope to acquire land in Holland. They resolved, therefore, to go to America. There, they thought, they could get farms for nothing. And their children would never forget the English language or the good old English customs and laws. By living in the wilderness, they would not only enjoy freedom to worship as they wanted, but they could build up a settlement that would be their own.

## The Pilgrims, with Captain Myles Standish, sail for England and then for America; they reach Cape Cod, and choose a governor there

In 1620, a company of Pilgrims sailed from Holland to England with the intent to go to America. Captain Myles Standish, an English soldier who had fought in Holland, joined them. He did not belong to the Pilgrim church, but he

---

3   There were some people in England who taught very much as the Pilgrims did in regard to religious beliefs, but they did not leave the Church of England as the Pilgrims did. Members of this latter group insisted on making certain changes in the English mode of worship and in its teachings. As they said, they wanted to *purify* the church. And so they were called Puritans. Many Puritans came to New England with Governor Winthrop in 1630. After they settled in America, they established independent churches like the Pilgrims.

Map 13. Pilgrim and Puritan landings in New England.

had become a great friend to those who did.

About a hundred of these people sailed from Plymouth, England, for the New World, in the ship *Mayflower*. Many of those who went were children and young people. The Pilgrims had a long, rough passage across the Atlantic. Toward the end of November (1620), they saw land. It was Cape Cod, a narrow strip of sand, more than 60 miles long, that looks like an arm bent at the elbow, with a hand like a half-shut fist.

Finding that it would be difficult to go further, the Pilgrims decided to land and explore the cape. So the Mayflower entered Cape Cod Harbor, inside the half-shut fist, and then came to anchor.

Before they landed, the Pilgrims held a meeting in the cabin, and drew up an agreement in writing for the government of the settlement. They signed the agreement, and then chose John Carver for governor.

### Washing-day; what Standish and his men found on the Cape

On the first Monday after they had reached the cape, all the women went on shore to wash, and so Monday has been kept as washing-day in New England ever since. Shortly after that, Captain Standish, with a number of men, started off to see the country. They found some Indian corn buried in the sand. A little further on, a young man named William Bradford[4] stepped into an Indian deer trap. It jerked him up by the leg in a way that must have made even the Pilgrims smile.

**Captain Standish and his men set sail in a boat for a blue hill in the west, and find Plymouth Rock; Plymouth Harbor; landing from the Mayflower**

The landing at Plymouth.

As the Mayflower remained anchored in Cape Cod Harbor, the people on board could see a blue hill, on the mainland in the west, about forty miles away. Captain Standish and some others determined to go to that blue hill. Taking a sailboat, they started off. A few days later they passed the hill, which the Indians called Manomet,[5] and entered a fine harbor. There, on December 21, 1620,—the shortest day in the year,—they landed on that famous stone which is now known all over the world as Plymouth Rock.

Standish, with the others, went back to the Mayflower with a good report. They had found just what they wanted,—an excellent harbor where ships from England could come in; a brook of nice drinking water; and, last of all, a piece of

---

4   William Bradford would later become governor of the Massachusetts Bay Colony.
5   Manomet (Man'o-met).

land that was nearly free from trees, so that nothing would hinder their planting corn early in the spring.

Captain John Smith of Virginia had been there before them, and had named the place Plymouth on his map of New England. The Pilgrims liked the name, and so they made up their minds to keep it. The *Mayflower* soon sailed for Plymouth, England, and the Pilgrims set to work to build the log cabins of their little settlement.

## Sickness and death

During that winter, nearly half the Pilgrims died. Captain Standish showed himself to be as good a nurse as he was a soldier. He, with Governor Carver and their minister, Elder Brewster, cooked, washed, waited on the sick, and did everything that kind hearts and willing hands could to help their suffering friends. But the men who had begun to build houses had to stop that work to dig graves. When these graves were filled, they were smoothed down flat so that no prowling Indian might count the bodies and determine how few newcomers there were left.

## Samoset,[6] Squanto,[7] and Massasoit[8] visit the Pilgrims

One day in the spring, the Pilgrims were startled when an Indian walked boldly into their little settlement. He cried out in good English, "Welcome! Welcome!" The visitor was named Samoset; he had met some sailors years before, and had learned a few English words from them.

The next time Samoset came, he brought with him another Indian, a man named Squanto. Squanto was the only one

6  Samoset (Sam'o-set).
7  Squanto (Skwon'tō).
8  Massasoit (Mas'uh-so'it).

left of the tribe that had once lived at Plymouth. All the rest had died of a dreadful sickness or plague. He had been stolen by some sailors and carried to England. There, he too had learned the English language. After his return, he had joined an Indian tribe that lived about thirty miles further west. The chief of that tribe was named Massasoit, and Squanto said that he was coming to visit the Pilgrims.

"Welcome! Welcome!"

In about an hour, Massasoit appeared on a hill just outside the settlement together with some 60 warriors. The Indians had painted their faces in their most festive style—black, red, and yellow. If paint could make them handsome, they were determined to look their best.

## Massasoit and Governor Carver make a treaty[9] of friendship; how Thanksgiving was kept; what Squanto did for the Pilgrims

Captain Standish, attended by a guard of honor, went out to meet the visitors and brought the chief to Governor Carver. Then Massasoit and the governor made a solemn promise—or treaty—in which they agreed that the Indians of Massasoit's tribe and the Pilgrims would live like friends and brothers; they would do all they could to help each other.

---

9  Treaty: an agreement.

That promise was kept for more than 50 years; it was never broken until long after the two men who made it were in their graves.

When the Pilgrims had their first Thanksgiving, they invited Massasoit and his men to come and share it. The Indians brought venison and other good things; there were plenty of wild turkeys roasted; and so they all sat down together to a great dinner, and had a merry time in the wilderness.

Squanto was of great help to the Pilgrims. He showed them how to catch eels, where to go fishing, when to plant their corn, and how to put a fish in every hill to make it grow fast.

After a while, he came to live with the Pilgrims. He liked them so much that when he died, he begged Governor Bradford to pray that he might go to the white man's heaven.

### Canonicus[10] dares Governor Bradford to fight; the palisade; the fort and meeting-house

West of where Massasoit lived, there were some Indians on the shore of Narragansett Bay.[11] This is in the area now known as Rhode Island. The tribal chief was named Canonicus, and he was no friend either to Massasoit or to the Pilgrims. Canonicus thought he could frighten the white men away, so he sent a

---

10 Canonicus (Kuh-non'ih-kus).
11 Narragansett (Nar'uh-gan'set): see Map 19, p. 78.

bundle of sharp, new arrows, tied round with a rattlesnake skin. He sent this package to Governor Bradford. The meaning was clear: he was daring the governor and his men to come out to fight.

Governor Bradford threw away the arrows, filled the snake-skin up to the mouth with powder and ball, and then sent all of this back to Canonicus. When Canonicus saw what Bradford had sent him, he was afraid to touch it, for he knew that Myles Standish's bullets would whistle louder and cut deeper than his Indian arrows.

But though the Pilgrims did not believe that Canonicus would attack them, they thought it best to build a very high, strong fence, called a palisade, around the town.

They also built a log fort on one of the hills, and used the lower part of the fort for a church building.

Every Sunday, all the people, with Captain Standish at the head, marched to their meetinghouse, where a man stood on guard outside. Each Pilgrim carried his gun, and set it down near him. With one ear he listened sharply to the preacher; with the other he listened just as sharply for the cry, Indians! Indians! But the Indians never came.

## The new settlers; conflict; Captain Standish's fight with Indians

By and by, more emigrants came from England and settled about 25 miles north of Plymouth, at what is now called Wey-

The palisade built round Plymouth.

57

mouth. The Indians who had been living in that neighbor-hood were not pleased to have these foreigners move into their territory uninvited, and they made up their minds to get them out of there.

Governor Bradford sent Captain Standish with nine men to see how great the danger was. Standish was surprised at the Indians' boldness. In one incident, a large Indian was said to have come up to him. Whetting a long knife, the man held it up to show how sharp it was. Then, gently patting it, he said, "By and by, it shall eat, but not speak."

Presently, another Indian came up. He, too, was a big man, much larger and stronger than Standish. And he, too, had a long knife. "Ah," Standish reported him as saying. "So this is the mighty captain the white men have sent to destroy us! He is a little man. Let him go and work with the women."[12]

The captain was on fire with rage; but said nothing.

The next day, Standish and the men with him requested a meeting with the Indians in a log cabin at Weymouth. Once the Indians were all inside, Standish made a sign to one of his men and the man shut and secured the cabin door. Then Standish sprang like a tiger at the larger of the two men who had mocked him, and used his own knife against him. A hand-to-hand fight followed between the white men and the Indians. The Pilgrims gained the victory, and carried the head of the Indian chief in triumph back to Plymouth.

For the Indians, of course, this was a terrible defeat and Standish's behavior created for these Indians a new word for the Pilgrims from Plymouth. Ever after, the Plymouth Pilgrims were called "Stabbers." The incident was seen dif-

---

12 According to the best historical records we have (coming, of course, from the Pilgrims' side!), the story and quotations here are truthful to the spirit of what occurred.

ferently, of course, from the Pilgrims' perspective. To them, Captain Standish had acted boldly and saved both of the English settlements from destruction.

## What else Myles Standish did; his death

Myles Standish did more things for the Pilgrims than fight for them. He went to England, bought goods for them, and borrowed money to help them.

He lived to be an old man. At his death, he left among other things three well-worn Bibles and three good guns. In those days, people said that the men who read the Bible most were those who fought the hardest.[13]

Near Plymouth there is a high hill called Captain's Hill. That is where Standish made his home during the last of his life. A granite monument over 100 feet high stands on top of the hill. On it is a statue of the brave captain looking toward the sea. He was one of the makers of modern America.

Myles Standish's kettle, sword, and pewter dish.

Myles Standish's signature.

---

13 The reason for such a saying is fairly obvious. This was the time when religious wars were common among the European nations. Those, of course, who "read the Bible most" were the most religiously committed—and, therefore, the most ready to "stand up for their scruples" (i.e., fight for the things they believed in)—among Protestant believers.

## Governor John Winthrop founds[14] Boston

In 1630, ten years after the Pilgrims landed at Plymouth, a large company of English people under the leadership of Governor John Winthrop came to New England. They were called Puritans,[15] and they, too, were seeking that religious freedom that was denied them in the old country. One of the vessels that brought over these new settlers was called the *Mayflower*. It is possible she was the very same ship that brought the Pilgrims to America ten years before.

Governor Winthrop's company named the place where they settled Boston, in grateful remembrance of the beautiful old city of Boston, England,[16] from which some of the chief emigrants came. The new settlement was called the Massachusetts Bay[17] Colony, Massachusetts being the Indian name for the Blue Hills near Boston.

The Plymouth Colony was now often called the Old Colony, because it had been settled first. After many years, these two colonies were united, and still later they became the State of Massachusetts.

## How other New England colonies grew up; the Revolution

By the time Governor Winthrop arrived, English settlements had been made in Maine, New Hampshire, and later (1724), in the country that afterward became the State of Vermont. Connecticut and Rhode Island were first settled by emigrants from Massachusetts.

---

14  Founds, begins to build.
15  See Footnote 3, p. 51.
16  Boston, England; see Map 12, p. 50.
17  Massachusetts Bay; see Map 16, p. 71.

When the Revolution broke out, the people throughout New England took up arms in defense of their rights. The first blood of the war was shed on the soil of Massachusetts, near Boston.

## Summary

The Pilgrims landed at Plymouth, New England, in 1620. One of the chief men who came with them was Captain Myles Standish. Had it not been for him, the Indians might have destroyed the English settlement. In 1630, Governor John Winthrop, with a large company of emigrants from England, settled Boston. The first battle of the American Revolution was fought near Boston.

## Questions

Why did some Englishmen in Holland call themselves Pilgrims?

Why had they left England?

Why did they want to go to America?

Who was Myles Standish?

From what place in England, and in what ship, did the Pilgrims sail?

What land did the Pilgrims first see in America?

What did they do after they arrived at Cape Cod Harbor but before anyone left the ship?

What did they do on the Cape?

Where did they land on December 21st, 1620?

What happened during the winter?

Who was Samoset?

What did he do?

And Squanto: who was he and what did he do?

And Massasoit: who was he and what did he and Governor Carver do?

What do you know about the first Thanksgiving?

Who was Canonicus and what did he do?

How did Governor Bradford respond to Canonicus?

What did the Pilgrims build to protect themselves from Indians?

What happened in Weymouth?

Besides fight, what else did Myles Standish do in behalf of the Plymouth Colony?

What did Governor John Winthrop do?

Where did the names *Boston* and *Massachusetts* come from?

What did the people of New England do in the Revolution?

Where was the first blood shed in the American Revolution?

# Lord Baltimore

## 1580-1632

**Lord Baltimore's settlement in Newfoundland;[1] how Catholics were then treated in England**

Map 14. Newfoundland.

While Captain Myles Standish was helping build up Plymouth, Lord Baltimore, an English nobleman, was trying to make a settlement on the cold, foggy island of Newfoundland.

Lord Baltimore had been brought up a Protestant, but had become a Catholic. At that time, Catholics were treated very cruelly in England. They were ordered by law to attend the Church of England. They did not like that church any better than the Pilgrims did. But if they failed to attend it, they had to take their choice between paying a large sum of money or going to prison.

Lord Baltimore hoped to make a home for himself and for other English Catholics in the wilderness of Newfoundland where there would be no one to trouble them. But the unfortunate settlers were nearly frozen out. They had winter a good portion of the year, and had to endure fog all of it.

---

1 Newfoundland (Noo'fund-lund).

They could grow nothing because, as one man said, the soil was either rock or swamp. The rock was as hard as iron; the swamp was so deep that you could not touch bottom with a ten-foot pole.

## The king of England gives Lord Baltimore part of Virginia, and names it Maryland; what Lord Baltimore paid for it

King Charles I of England was a good friend to Lord Baltimore. When Baltimore and his co-settlers gave up their land in Newfoundland, Charles made him a present of an immense three-cornered piece of land in America. This piece was cut out of Virginia, north of the Potomac[2] River.

The king's wife, Queen Mary, was a French Catholic. Charles named the country he had given Lord Baltimore, Mary Land, or Maryland—in his wife's

Part of Windsor Castle.

honor. He could not have chosen a better name, because Maryland was to be a shelter for many English people who believed in the same religion that the queen did.

All that Lord Baltimore had to pay for Maryland, with its 12,000 square miles of land and water, was two Indian arrows. These he agreed to send every spring to the royal palace at Windsor[3] Castle, near London.

---

2   Potomac (Puh-to'muk): see Map 23, p. 120.
3   Windsor (Win'zer).

The arrows would be worth nothing whatever to the king; but they were sent as a kind of yearly rent. They showed that, though Lord Baltimore had the use of Maryland, and could do pretty much as he pleased with it, still the king did not give up all control of it.

In Virginia and in New England, the king had granted all land to companies of persons, and he had been particular to tell them just what they must or must not do. Maryland, however, he gave to one man only. More than this, he promised to let Lord Baltimore have his own way in everything, as long as he made no laws in Maryland that would be contrary to the laws of England. So Lord Baltimore had greater privileges than any other holder of land in America at that time.

The landing in Maryland.

### Lord Baltimore dies; his son sends emigrants to Maryland; the landing; the Indians; St. Mary's

Lord Baltimore died before he was able to go to America. His eldest son, then, became Lord Baltimore in his stead. The son sent over a number of emigrants. Some of them were Catholics and some were Protestants. All of them were to have equal rights in Maryland.

In the spring of 1634, these people landed on a little island near the mouth of the Potomac River. There they cut down

Map 15. Maryland.

a tree, and made a large cross of it. Then, kneeling round that cross, they all joined in a prayer of thanks to God for their safe journey.

A little later, they landed on the shore of the river. There they met Indians. Under a huge mulberry tree they bargained with the Indians for a place to build a town, and they paid for the land in hatchets, knives, and beads.

The Indians were greatly astonished at the size of the ship in which the white men came. They thought that it was made like their canoes, out of the trunk of a tree hollowed out, and they wondered where the English could have found a tree big enough to make it.

The emigrants named their settlement St. Mary's, because they had landed on a day kept sacred to the Virgin Mary.[4] The Indians gave up one of their largest wigwams to Father White, one of the priests who had come over, and he made a church of it. It was the first English Catholic Church opened in America.

The Indians and the settlers lived and worked together side by side. The Indian men showed the emigrants how to hunt in the forest, and the Indian women taught the English women how to make hominy[5] and how to bake johnny-cakes[6] before the open fire.

---

4  March 25th: Annunciation or Lady Day; the day Christians celebrate the Annunciation—or Announcement—to Mary by an angel that she was to bear a son named Jesus who would be called the Son of God. See Luke 1:26-38 in the Bible.
5  Hominy: coarsely ground corn used to make grits.
6  Johnny-cake: cornmeal bread cooked in the shape of a pancake.

## Maryland the home of religious liberty

Maryland was different from the other English colonies in America because there, and there only, every Christian, whether Catholic or Protestant, had the right to worship God in his own way. In that humble little village of St. Mary's, made up of 30 or 40 log huts and wigwams, "religious liberty had its only home in the wide world."

But more than this, Lord Baltimore generously invited people who had been driven out of the other settlements on account of their religion to come and live in Maryland. He gave a hearty welcome to all, whether they thought as he did or not. And so he showed that he was a noble man by nature as well as a nobleman by name.

## Maryland falls into trouble; the city of Baltimore built

Sadly, the happy state of things did not last long in Maryland. Some of the people of Virginia were very angry because the king had given Lord Baltimore part of what they thought was their land. They quarreled with the new settlers and made them a great deal of trouble.

Then worse things happened. Men from Virginia went to Maryland in order to drive out the Catholics. In some cases they acted in a very shameful manner toward Lord Baltimore and his friends. Among other things, they put Father White in irons and sent him back to England as a prisoner.

Lord Baltimore had spent a great deal of money in building up the settlement, but his right to the land was taken away from him for a time, and all who dared to defend him were badly treated.

St. Mary's never grew to be much of a place, but not quite a hundred years after the English landed there, in 1729, Marylanders started a new and beautiful city. They named it Baltimore, in honor of the Lord Baltimore who sent out the first emigrants.

## Summary

King Charles I of England gave Lord Baltimore, an English Catholic, a part of Virginia and named it Maryland. He named it Maryland in honor of his wife, Queen Mary. A company of emigrants moved to Maryland in 1634. Maryland was the first settlement in America in which all Christian people had entire liberty to worship God in whatever way they thought right. That liberty they owed to Lord Baltimore.

## Questions

Who was Lord Baltimore, and what did he try to do in Newfoundland?

How were Catholics then treated in England?

What did the king of England give Lord Baltimore in America?

What did the king name the country?

What was Lord Baltimore required to pay for Maryland?

What did the king promise Lord Baltimore?

What did Lord Baltimore's son do?

When and where did the emigrants land?

What did they call the place?

The Indians were surprised at the size of the English people's boat. Why?

Maryland became known as the home of a certain kind of liberty. What was it?

Why did some of the people of Virginia trouble the residents of Maryland?

How did the city of Baltimore get its name?

# Roger Williams

1600-1684

**Roger Williams comes to Boston; he preaches in Salem and in Plymouth; his friendship for the Indians**

The church in which Roger Williams preached in Salem.

Shortly after Governor John Winthrop and his company settled Boston, a young minister named Roger Williams came from England to join them.

Mr. Williams soon became a great friend to the Indians and while he preached at Salem[1] and at Plymouth, he came to know many of them. He took pains to learn their language, and he spent a great deal of time talking with chief Massasoit and his men, in their smoky wigwams. He made the Indians feel that, as he said, he desired to do them good. For this reason they were always glad to see him and ready to help him. A time came, as we shall presently see, when they were able to do quite as much for him as he could for them.

---

1   Salem: see Map 16, p. 71.

## Who owned the greater part of America? what the king of England thought; what Roger Williams thought and said

The company that had settled Boston held the land by permission of the king of England. He considered that most of the land in America belonged to him, because John Cabot had discovered it.

But Roger Williams said that the king had no right to the land unless he bought it from the Indians who were living there when the English came.

Now the people of Massachusetts were always quite willing to pay the Indians a fair price for whatever land they wanted, but many of them were afraid to have Mr. Williams preach and write as he did. They believed that if they allowed him to go on speaking out so boldly against the king, the English monarch would get so angry that he would take away Massachusetts from them and give it to a new company. In that case, those who had settled here would lose everything. For this reason, the people of Boston tried to make the young minister agree to keep silent on this subject.

## A constable is sent to arrest Roger Williams; he escapes to the woods, and goes to Mount Hope

Mr. Williams was not one to keep silent, despite the pleas of his neighbors. If he believed something was true, then he would speak it.

The leading men of Boston eventually sent a constable up to Salem. They had orders to seize Williams and to send him back to England. When he heard that the constable was after him, Mr. Williams slipped quietly out of his house and escaped to the woods.

There was a heavy depth of snow on the ground, but the young man made up his mind that he would go to his old friend Massasoit, and ask him to help him in his trouble.

Map 16. Roger Williams's route from Salem to Mount Hope.

Massasoit lived near Mount Hope, in what is now Rhode Island, about 80 miles southwest from Salem. There were no roads through the woods, and it was a long, dreary journey to make on foot, but Mr. Williams did not hesitate. He took a hatchet to chop fire-wood, a flint and steel to strike a fire, and a pocket-compass to aid him in finding his way through the thick forest.

All day he waded wearily on through the deep snow, only stopping now and then to rest or to look at his compass and make sure that he was going in the right direction. At night he would gather wood enough to make a little fire to warm himself or to melt some snow for drink. Then he would

Striking fire with flint and steel. The sparks were caught on some old, half-burnt rag, and were then blown to a blaze.

cut down a few boughs for a bed, or, if he was lucky enough to find a large, hollow tree, he would creep into that. There he would fall asleep, while listening to the howling of the wind or to the fiercer howling of the hungry wolves prowling about the woods.

At length, after much suffering from cold and lack of food, he managed to reach Massasoit's wigwam. There, the big-hearted Indian chief gave him a warm welcome. He took him into his cabin and kept him till spring. He required Williams to pay him no board. All the Indians liked the young minister. Even Canonicus, the chief of a neighboring tribe who had dared Governor Bradford to fight, said that he loved Williams "as his own son."

## Roger Williams at Seekonk;[2] "What cheer, friend?"

"What cheer, friend?"

When the warm days came, in the spring of 1636, Mr. Williams began building a log hut for himself at Seekonk, on the east bank of the Seekonk River. But he was told that his cabin stood on ground owned by the people of Massachusetts. So, together with a few friends who had joined him, Williams took a canoe and paddled downstream to find a new place to build.

"What cheer, friend? What cheer?" shouted some Indians who were standing on a rock on the western bank of the river. That was the Indian way of saying How do you do, and just then Roger Williams was glad to hear it.

---

2  Seekonk (See'konk): See Map 17, p. 73.

He landed on what is now called "What Cheer Rock,"[3] and had a talk with the Indians. They told him that there was a fine spring of water round the point of land a little further down. He went there, and liked the spot so much that he decided to stop. His friend Canonicus owned the land, and he gladly let Williams have what he needed. Williams

Map 17. Seekonk, What Cheer Rock and Providence.

believed that a kind Providence had guided him to this pleasant place, and for this reason he named it Providence.

Providence was the first settlement in America that set its doors wide open to everyone who wanted to come and live there. Not only all Christians, but Jews, and even people who went to no church whatever, could go there and be at peace.

This was the work of Roger Williams. In time, Providence grew to be the chief city in the State of Rhode Island.

## Summary

Roger Williams, a young minister of Salem, Massachusetts, declared that the Indians, and not the king of England, owned the land in America. The governor of Massachusetts was afraid that if Mr. Williams kept on saying these things, the king would hear of it and would take away the land held by the people of Boston and the other settlements. The governor therefore sent a constable to arrest the young minister and put him on board a ship going back to England. When Mr. Williams heard of this, he fled to the Indian chief, Mas-

---

3 "What Cheer Rock" is on the east side of the city of Providence.

sasoit. In 1636 Roger Williams began building Providence in what is now known as the State of Rhode Island. Providence was the first settlement in America that offered a home to anyone without asking them anything whatever about their religious beliefs.

## Questions

Who was Roger Williams?

He held a very different attitude toward the Indians than did the other English people around him. What was that?

How did many of the people of Massachusetts feel about Williams?

What did the leaders of Boston do?

When he heard of the leaders' plan, what did Williams do?

Describe Williams' journey to Mount Hope.

What did Massasoit do for Williams?

Williams began to build a cabin at Seekonk but then quit. Why?

What happened after that?

Why did Williams name his new settlement Providence?

What is unique about Providence?

# King Philip

Time of the Indian War, 1675-1676

## Death of Massasoit; Wamsutta[1] and Metacomet;[2] Wamsutta's sudden death

When the Indian chief Massasoit died, the people of Plymouth lost one of their best friends. Massasoit left two sons named Wamsutta and Metacomet. Wamsutta was the older and he took over the leadership role of his father. The two younger men both lived near Mount Hope, in Rhode Island.

The governor of Plymouth heard that Wamsutta was stirring up the Indians to make war on the whites. So he sent men to bring the Indian chief to him at gunpoint so Wamsutta could give an account of himself. Wamsutta came, but on his way back, he suffered a sudden "illness" that led to his death soon after he reached home.

Considering the circumstances of the illness and the distrust brewing between the Indians and the English settlers, it ought to surprise no one that Wamsutta's wife and his brother Metacomet both claimed the white colonists had poisoned him. The charge has never been proven true or false, but the Indians certainly believed it.

---

1　Wamsutta (Wam-sut'uh).
2　Metacomet (Meh-tah'com-it)

## How Metacomet became "King Philip"; why he hated the white men; how the white men got possession of the Indian lands

When their father, Massasoit, died, Wamsutta and Metacomet commemorated the event by adopting the English

The belt King Philip wore as a kind of crown.

names their father had chosen for them. Wamsutta took the name Alexander and Metacomet took the name Philip. Wamsutta didn't live long enough for his English name to be commonly known. But when he died, Metacomet became chief and the English settlers soon recognized him by his English name: King Philip.

Philip lived in a wigwam of bark. On great occasions he wore a bright red blanket and a crown made of a broad belt ornamented with shells. Because he was convinced that the English had murdered his brother, and because he saw

Map 18. Territory of the Wampanoag nation.

that the English settlers were growing stronger in numbers every year, Philip adopted a policy of opposition.

When the Pilgrims landed at Plymouth, Massasoit, Philip's father, was leader of the Wampanoag nation, the people that lived from Cape Cod west to the eastern shores of Narragansett Bay, a strip of land about 30 miles wide. The white settlers bought a small piece of this land. After a while they bought more, and so they kept on until in about 50 years they had acquired nearly all of what Massasoit's tribe had once owned. The Indians had nothing left but two little necks of land that were nearly surrounded by the waters of Narragansett Bay. Here they felt that they were shut up almost like prisoners, and that the white men watched everything they did.

## How King Philip felt; signs of the coming war; the "Praying Indians"; a murder

King Philip was a very proud man—quite as proud, in fact, as the king of England. He could not bear to see his people losing power. He said to himself, if the Indians do not rise and drive out the white men, then the white men will certainly drive out the Indians.

Most of the Indians now had guns, and could use them quite as well as the whites could. So Philip thought it best to fight.

The settlers sensed that a war was coming. Some of them said they saw the figure of an Indian bow in the clouds. Others said they heard sounds like guns fired off in the air, and horsemen riding furiously up and down in the sky, as if getting ready for battle.

But though many Indians now hated the white settlers, this was not true of all. A minister named John Eliot had persuaded some of the Indians near Boston to give up their religion and to try to live like the English people. These were called "Praying Indians." One of them, who knew King Philip well, told the settlers that Philip's warriors were grinding their hatchets in preparation for war. King Philip was brought before a colonial court to answer the charges. Of course, there was no proof that Philip was doing what the informer had said. But the court warned Philip that any similar rumors, whether true or not, would lead to confiscation of Wampanoag land and guns.

Soon after this incident, the "Praying Indian" informer was found murdered. Some English colonists accused three of Philip's men of having killed him. The three were tried before a jury of English and Indian men, found guilty, and hanged.

## Beginning of war at Swansea;[3] burning of Brookfield

Map 19. The territory of "King Philip's War."

King Philip's warriors launched an attack in the summer of 1675. Some white settlers were going home from church in the town of Swansea, Massachusetts. They had been to pray that there might be no fighting. As they walked along, talking together, two guns were fired out of the bushes. One of the white men fell dead in the road, and another was badly hurt.

---

3 Swansea (Swon'zee).

The shots were fired by Indians. This was the way they always fought when they could. They were not cowards, but they preferred to attack from behind trees and rocks. By such means, a man could be killed without seeing who shot him.

Indian attack on a village.

At first, fighting occurred in those villages of Plymouth Colony that were nearest Narragansett Bay. Then it spread to the valley of the Connecticut River and its neighborhood. Deerfield, Springfield, Brookfield, Groton,[4] and many other places in Massachusetts were attacked. The Indians would creep up stealthily in the night, burn the houses, carry off the women and children as prisoners if they could, kill the rest of the inhabitants, and take their scalps home to hang in their wigwams.[5]

At Brookfield the settlers left their houses and gathered in one strong house for defense. The Indians burned all the abandoned houses, and did their best to burn the occupied house as well.

---

4   Groton (Graw'tun).
5   Scalping: Lest we read this as a particularly gruesome and evil act on the part of King Philip's men, we should understand the context. According to James Axtell, a professor of history at the College of William & Mary in Virginia, the practice of scalping was common long before Christopher Columbus arrived.

They dipped rags in sulfur, such as what we use to make matches, fastened these sulfured rags to the points of their arrows, set fire to them, and shot the blazing arrows into the shingles of the roof.

When the Indians saw that the shingles were beginning to flame, they danced for joy and shouted in triumph. But the men in the house somehow managed to put out the fire on the roof.

At that, the Indians got a cart, filled it with hay, set it on fire, and pushed it up against the house. This time they thought for sure they would burn the settlers out. But just then, a heavy shower came and put the fire out. Shortly after, some English soldiers marched into the village, and saved the people in the house.

## The fight at Hadley; what Colonel[6] Goffe[7] did

At Hadley, the English colonists were in their meeting-house when an Indian war-whoop[8] rang through the village. The Indians drove back those who went out against them, and it seemed as if the village would be destroyed. Suddenly, a white-haired old Englishman, sword in hand, appeared among the settlers. No one knew who he was; but he called to them to follow him, as a captain calls to his men, and they obeyed. The astonished Indians turned and ran.

When all was over, the settlers looked for their brave leader and couldn't find him. He had gone. They never saw him again. Many thought that he was an angel who had been sent to save them. But it turned out their "angel" was Colonel

---

6  Colonel (ker′nul): the chief officer of a regiment of soldiers.
7  Goffe (Gof).
8  War-whoop: a very loud, shrill cry made by the Indians when engaged in war, or as a shout of alarm.

Goffe, one of the judges who had signed the death warrant for English King Charles I at the end of the second English Civil War.[9] Goffe had risen to prominence during the years after the war. But when Charles II was restored to power,[10]

Colonel Goffe's brave leadership.

Goffe had had to flee in order to save his life. Luckily for the people of Hadley, he was hiding there in the house of a friend when the Indians attacked the village.

## How a woman drove off an Indian

In this dreadful war with the Indians, there were times when even the women had to fight for their lives. In one case, a woman had been left in a house with two young children. She heard a noise at the window, and looking up, saw an

---

9   English Civil War (1642–1651): a series of conflicts between supporters of the English Parliament (Parliamentarians; also known as Roundheads) against supporters of the King (Royalists; also known as Cavaliers). The war led to the execution of Charles I, the exile of his son, Charles II, and replacement of English monarchy with, first, a republican form of government, called the Commonwealth of England (1649–53), and then with military dictatorship, called the Protectorate (1653–59), under Oliver Cromwell and, briefly, his son, Richard.

10  Restoration of the English monarchy (1660): When Oliver Cromwell died in 1658, the English government soon fell into disarray. When no one else showed a strong ability to rule, Charles II, who was living in exile in the Spanish Netherlands, eventually issued what is known as the Declaration of Breda. The Declaration promised a general pardon for crimes committed during the English Civil War and the period following for all those who would recognize Charles as the lawful king. All would be pardoned except the men who had signed the death warrant for Charles I. The Declaration offered several other promises that were valuable to those who heard them. And so, with these promises in hand, Parliament passed a resolution that "government ought to be by King, Lords and Commons." They invited Charles to return to England to receive his crown. On May 8, Charles was proclaimed King.

Indian attack on
a settlement.

The building on the
right is a blockhouse,
or fort made of hewn
logs. These block-
houses were built as
places of refuge for the
settlers, in case of an
attack on the town by
the Indians.

Indian trying to raise the sash. Quick as thought, she clapped the two little children under two large brass kettles, then, seizing a shovel-full of red-hot coals from the open fire, she stood ready, and, just as the Indian thrust his head into the room, she dashed the coals into his face and eyes. With a yell of agony the Indian let go his hold, dropped to the ground, and ran howling into the woods.

## The great swamp fight; burning the Indian wigwams; what the Chief Canonchet[11] said

During the summer and autumn of 1675, the Indians on the west side of Narragansett Bay[12] took no open part in King Philip's War. But the next winter, the English settlers found evidence that these Indians were secretly receiving and sheltering the men who had been wounded in fighting for King Philip. And so the settlers determined to raise a large force and attack them.

The Indians had gathered in a fort on an island in a swamp. This fort was a very difficult place to reach. It was built of the trunks of trees set upright in the ground. It was so strong that the Indians felt quite safe.

Starting very early in the morning, the attacking party waded fifteen miles through deep snow. Many of them had their hands and feet badly frozen. One of the chief men in leading the attack was Captain Benjamin Church of Plymouth; he was a very brave soldier, and knew all about Indian life and Indian fighting. In the battle, he was struck by two bullets, and so badly wounded that he could not move a step further. He made one of his men hold him up and he shouted to his soldiers to go ahead. The fight was a desperate one, but

---

11 Canonchet (Kuh-non'shut).
12 Narragansett: See Map 19, p. 78.

at length the fort was taken. The attacking party lost more than 250 men either killed or wounded. The Indians lost as many as a thousand.

After the battle was over, Captain Church begged the men not to burn the wigwams inside the fort, for there were a great number of old men, women, and little children inside the wigwams. But his men were very angry and would not listen to him. They set the wigwams on fire, and burned many of these people to death.

Canonchet, the chief of the tribe, was taken prisoner. The settlers told him they would spare his life if he would try to make peace. "No," he said. "We will all fight to the last man rather than become slaves to the white men." He was then told that he would be shot. "I like it well," he said. "I wish to die before my heart becomes soft, or I say anything unworthy of myself."

## Philip's wife and son are taken prisoners; Philip is shot; end of the war

The next summer, Captain Church, with a lot of men from Bridgewater, chased King Philip and his men. They took many of the Indians prisoner. Among those taken were King Philip's wife and little boy. When Philip heard of it, he cried out, "My heart breaks. Now I am ready to die."

He had good reason to say so.

It was the custom in England to sell prisoners of war as slaves. Following this custom, the settlers took this boy, the grandson of Massasoit, the man who had helped them when they were poor and weak, and they sold him with his mother into slavery. The boy and his mother were sent to the

Bermuda Islands,[13] and there worked to death under the hot sun and the lash of a slave-driver's whip.

Not long after that, King Philip himself was shot. He had been hunted like an animal from place to place. At last he had come back to see his old home at Mount Hope[14] once more. There Captain Church found him. And there the Indian warrior was shot.

King Philip's death brought the war to an end. It had lasted a little over a year—from the early summer of 1675 to the latter part of the summer of 1676. In that short time the Indians had killed over 600 white settlers, and had burned 12 villages to ashes, besides partly burning a great many more. The war cost the New England colonists over £100,000—a significant amount of money at a time when most families earned less than £20 per year. But however much the colonists lost, the Indians lost more. Their strength was

Death of King Philip.

---

13 Bermuda: the Bermuda Islands are in the Atlantic, north of the West India Islands and east of South Carolina; they belong to Great Britain.

14 Mount Hope: See Map 16, p. 71.

broken, and they never dared to trouble the people of Southern New England again.

## Summary

In 1675, King Philip began a great Indian war against the people of Southeastern New England. His object was to kill off the white settlers, and get back the land for the Indians. His forces did kill a large number, and they destroyed many villages, but in the end, the English settlers gained the victory. Philip's wife and child were sold as slaves, and he was shot. The Indians never again attempted another war in New England.

## Questions

Who was Wamsutta?

What happened to him?

Who was King Philip?

Why was he opposed to the English settlers?

Who were the "Praying Indians" and what role did they play in King Philip's War?

What happened to one of them?

What did the English colonists then do to three of Philip's men?

Where and how did the war begin?

To what part of the country did it spread?

Tell about the Indian attack on Brookfield.

What happened at Hadley?

How did an English woman drive off an Indian attacker?

Tell all you can about the Great Swamp Fight and what the English settlers did afterward.

Who was Canonchet and what did he say?

What happened to King Philip's wife and son?

What happened to King Philip himself?

What was the result of the war?

# William Penn

1644-1718

## King Charles II gives William Penn a great piece of land, and names it Pennsylvania

William Penn at the age of 22.

King Charles II of England owed a large sum of money to a young Englishman named William Penn. The king was fond of pleasure, and he spent so much money on himself and his friends that he had none left to pay his debts. Penn knew this, so he told His Majesty that if he would give him a piece of wild land in America, he would ask nothing more.

Charles was very glad to settle the account so easily. He therefore gave Penn a great territory north of Maryland and west of the Delaware River. This territory was nearly as large as England. The king named it Pennsylvania,[1] a word that means Penn's Woods.

---

1 Pennsylvania: See Map 20, p. 89.

At that time, no one thought the land was worth much. No one had discovered that beneath Penn's Woods there were immense quantities of coal and iron which would one day be of greater value than all the riches of the king of England.

## William Penn's religion; what he wanted to do with his American land

Penn belonged to a religious group called the Society of Friends. Today they are generally spoken of as Quakers. They are a people who try to find out what is right by asking their own hearts. They believe in showing no more signs of respect to one man than to another, and, at that time, they wouldn't take off their hats even to the king himself.

William Penn receiving the Grant of Pennsylvania from Charles II.

Penn wanted the land that had been given him as a place where the Friends, or Quakers, might go and settle. A little later, the whole of what is now the State of New Jersey was bought by Penn and other Quakers for the same purpose.

We have seen that neither the Pilgrims nor the Catholics had any real peace in England. The Quakers suffered even more. Oftentimes, they were whipped cruelly and thrown into dark and dirty prisons where many died from the bad treatment they received.

William Penn himself had been shut up in jail four times on account of his religion. And though he was no longer in such danger, because the king was his friend, still, he wanted to provide a safe place for others who were not so well off as he was.

Map 20. Wilmington, Elizabeth and Philadelphia.

**Penn sends out emigrants to Pennsylvania; he gets ready to go himself; his conversation with the king**

In keeping with his desire to provide a refuge for Quakers, Penn sent to Pennsylvania a number of people who were anxious to settle there. The next year, 1682, he made ready to sail himself together with a hundred more emigrants. Just before he started, he called on the king in his palace in London. The king was fond of joking, and he said to Penn that he expected never to see him again since he thought the Indians would be sure to catch such a good-looking young man as Penn and eat him.

"But, Friend Charles," Penn replied, "I mean to buy the land of the Indians, so they will rather keep on good terms with me than eat me."

"Buy their lands!" exclaimed the king. "Why, is not the whole of America mine?"

"Certainly not," answered Penn.

"What!" replied the king. "Didn't my people discover it? And so haven't I the right to it?"

"Well, Friend Charles," said Penn, "suppose a canoe full of Indians should cross the sea and discover England. Would that make it theirs? Would you give up the country to them?"

The king did not know what to say to this; it was a new way of looking at the matter. He probably said to himself, "These Quakers are a strange people; they seem to think that even American Indians have rights that should be respected."

## Penn founds the city of Philadelphia; his treaty with the Indians; his visit to them; how the Indians and the Quakers got on together

When William Penn reached America in 1682, he sailed up the broad and beautiful Delaware River for nearly 20 miles. There he stopped, and resolved to build a city on its banks.

Penn making the treaty with the Indians.

He gave the place the Greek name of Philadelphia, or City of Brotherly Love. He hoped all of its citizens would live together like brothers.

Penn named the streets based on the trees then growing on the land, and so, even, today you can find streets in Philadelphia named Walnut, Pine, Cedar, Vine, and so on.

Penn said, "We intend to sit down lovingly among the Indians." On that account, he held a great meeting with them under a wide-spreading elm. The tree stood in what is now a part of Philadelphia. Here Penn and the Indians made a treaty by which they promised each other that they would live together as friends "as long as the water should run in the rivers, or the sun shine in the sky."

Nearly a hundred years later, while the Revolutionary War was going on, the British army took possession of the city. It was cold, winter weather, and the men wanted firewood. But the English general thought so much of William Penn that he set a guard of soldiers round the great elm to prevent anyone from chopping it down.

Not long after the great meeting under the elm, Penn visited some of the Indians in their wigwams. They treated him to a dinner of roasted acorns. After their feast, some of the young men began to run and leap about, to show the Englishman what they could do.

When Penn was in college at Oxford he had been fond of doing such things himself. The sight of the Indian boys made him feel like a boy again, too; so he sprang up from the ground, and beat them all at hop, skip, and jump. This completely won the hearts of the men who were there.

From that time, and for 60 years, the Pennsylvania settlers and the Indians kept their words of peace. The Indians said, "The Quakers are honest men; they do no harm; they are welcome to come here." In New England there had been, as we have seen, a terrible war with the Indians, but in Pennsylvania, no Indian ever shed a drop of Quaker blood.

## How Philadelphia grew; what happened there in the Revolution; William Penn's last years and death

Philadelphia grew quite fast. William Penn let the people have land very inexpensively, and he said to them, "You shall be governed by laws of your own making." Even after Philadelphia became quite a good-sized town, it had no poorhouse, for none was needed. Everyone seemed able to take care of himself.

When the American Revolution began, the people of Pennsylvania and of the colonies north and south of it sent men to Philadelphia to decide what should be done. This meeting of representatives from the North American colonies was called the Congress.[2] It was held in the old Pennsylvania State House, a building that still stands. In 1776, the Congress of the United States of America declared their states independent of England. In the war, the people of Delaware and New Jersey fought side by side with those of Pennsylvania.

William Penn spent a great deal of money to help Philadelphia and other settlements. After he returned to England, he was put in prison for debt by a rascally fellow he had employed. He did not owe the money, and proved that the

---

2  Congress: this word means a meeting or assembly of persons. The General, or Continental, Congress was an assembly of men who came from all of the 13 American colonies. They met at Philadelphia (and sometimes Baltimore) to decide what the colonies should do together. The first Congress at Philadelphia met in 1774, shortly before the Revolution began. After that, they met from time to time until near the close of the Revolution.

man who said he did was no better than a thief. Penn was released from prison; but his long confinement in jail had broken his health. When he died, the Indians of Pennsylvania sent his widow some beautiful furs, in remembrance of their "Brother Penn." They said that the furs were to make her a cloak, "to protect her while passing through this thorny wilderness without her guide."

William Penn in prison.

About 25 miles west of London, on a country road within sight of the towers of Windsor Castle, there stands a Friends' meeting-house, or Quaker church. William Penn lies buried in the yard behind the meeting-house. For a hundred years or more there was no mark of any kind to show where his body rests; but now a small stone bearing his name points out the grave of the founder of the great State of Pennsylvania.

## Summary

Charles II, king of England, owed William Penn, a young English Quaker, a large sum of money. In order to settle the debt, the king gave Penn a great piece of land in America, and named it Pennsylvania, or Penn's Woods. Penn wished to make a home for Quakers in America, and in 1682 he went to Pennsylvania and began building the city of Philadelphia. When the American Revolution broke out, men were sent from all the colonies to Philadelphia, to hold a meeting called the Congress. In 1776, Congress declared that the American British colonies it represented were now united in their resolve to be independent of British rule.

## Questions

To whom did King Charles II owe a large sum of money?

How did he pay his debt?

What did the king name the land that he gave?

What does the name mean?

What valuable resources have been found there?

Who or what are the Friends or Quakers?

For what did William Penn want the land the king gave him?

At the time the king gave his grant, how were the Quakers treated in England?

Penn determined to visit his lands in 1682. What did the king say to him as they were parting—and what did Penn say in reply?

What city did Penn begin to build in Pennsylvania?

What does the name Philadelphia mean?

Penn met with the Indians from the area. What did they do when they met?

Penn and the Indians met under a great elm tree. During the American Revolution, what did an English general do with respect to the elm ... and why?

What happened when Penn ate dinner with the Indians?

Did the Indians trouble the Quakers?

What happened in Philadelphia at the start of the American Revolution?

Tell what you can about Penn's last days.

Where is he buried?

# General James Oglethorpe
## 1696-1785

Map 21. Major cities in the southern colonies of North America.

**The twelve English colonies in America; General Oglethorpe makes a settlement in Georgia**

We have seen that the first real colony or settlement made in America by the English was in Virginia in 1607. By the beginning of 1733, or about 125 years later, 11 more had been made, or 12 in all. They stretched along the sea-coast, from the farthest coast of Maine to the northern boundary of Florida, which was then owned by the Spaniards.

The two colonies farthest south were North Carolina and South Carolina. In 1733, James Oglethorpe, a brave English soldier came to America to make a new settlement. This new one, which made 13 in all,[1] was called Georgia in honor

---

1  These 13 colonies or settlements were: First, the four New England colonies (New Hampshire, Massachusetts, Connecticut, and Rhode island; Maine was then part of Massachusetts, and Vermont was claimed by both New Hampshire and New York). Secondly, four middle colonies (New York, New Jersey, Pennsylvania, and Delaware). Thirdly, five southern colonies (Maryland, Virginia, North Carolina, South Carolina, and Georgia).

of King George II. King George gave a piece of land for it below South Carolina.

## What led General Oglethorpe to make this new settlement

General Oglethorpe had a friend in England who was cast into prison for debt. There the unfortunate man was so cruelly treated that he fell sick and died, leaving his family in great distress.

The General felt the death of his friend so much that he set to work to find out how other poor debtors were treated in the London prisons. He soon saw that great numbers of them suffered terribly. The prisons were crowded and filthy. The men shut up in them were ragged and dirty. Some of them were fastened with heavy chains, and a good many actually died of starvation.

General Oglethorpe could not bear to see strong men killed off in this manner. He thought that if the best of them—those who were honest and willing to work—were given the chance to earn their living, they would soon do as well as any men. It was to help these "worthy poor" that he persuaded the king to give the land of Georgia.

## Building the city of Savannah; what the people of Charleston, South Carolina, did; a busy settlement; the alligators

General Oglethorpe took 35 families to America in 1733. They settled on a high bank of the Savannah River, about 20 miles from the sea. The general laid out a town with broad, straight, handsome streets, and with many small squares or parks. He called the settlement Savannah from the Indian name of the river on which it would stand.

The people of Charleston, South Carolina, were glad to have some English neighbors south of them who would help them fight the Spaniards of Florida. After all, the Spaniards held no friendship for the English. Indeed, they wanted to drive the English out. So the Charlestonians gave their new neighbors a hundred head of cattle, a drove[2] of hogs, and 20 barrels of rice.

Laying out the city of Savannah.

The emigrants set to work with a will, cutting down the forest trees, building houses, and planting gardens. There were no idlers to be seen at Savannah. Even the children found something to do that was helpful.

Nothing disturbed the people but the alligators. They climbed up the bank from the river to see what was going on. But the boys soon taught them not to be too curious. When one monster was found impudently prowling around the town, the boys thumped him with sticks till they fairly beat the life out of him. After that, the alligators paid no more visits to the settlers.

---

2  Drove: one of the words for a group of hogs. (English has other unique words to describe groups of animals: a pride of lions; a flock of sheep; a colony of penguins; and so forth.)

The "blazed" trees.

## Arrival of some German emigrants; "Ebenezer"; "blazing" trees

After a time, some German Protestants came to Georgia. They had been driven out of their native land because of their religion. General Oglethorpe gave them a hearty welcome. He had bought land from the Indians, so there was plenty of room for all.

The Germans went up the river, and then went back a number of miles into the woods. There they picked out a place for a town. They called their settlement Ebenezer,[3] which means "Stone of help."

There were no roads through the forests, so the new settlers blazed the trees; that is, they chopped a piece of bark off, so that they could find their way through the thick woods when they wanted to go to Savannah. Every tree so marked stood like a guide-post. By looking for the blazed trees, travelers could tell which way they needed to go: find the next blazed tree and walk toward it.

---

3   Ebenezer (Eb-eh-nee'zer). See I Samuel 7:12 in the Bible for the name's source.

## Trying to make silk; the queen's American dress

The settlers hoped to be able to get large quantities of silk to send to England, because the mulberry-tree grows wild in Georgia, and its leaves are the favorite food of the silkworm.[4] At first it seemed as if the plan would be successful, and General Oglethorpe took over some Georgia silk as a present to the queen of England. She had a handsome dress made of it for her birthday. It was the first American silk dress ever worn by an English queen. But after a while, the colonists discovered silk could not be produced in Georgia anywhere near as easily as it could in Italy and France. And so, in time, the colonists abandoned silk in favor of cotton instead.

## Keeping out the Spaniards; Georgia powder at Bunker Hill; General Oglethorpe in his old age

The people of Georgia did a good work in keeping out the Spaniards, who were trying to get possession of the part of the country north of Florida. Later, like the settlers in North Carolina and South Carolina, they did their part in helping to make America independent of the rule of the king of England.

When the war of the Revolution began, the king had a lot of powder stored in Savannah. The people broke into the building, rolled out the kegs, and carried them off. Part of the powder they kept for themselves, and part they seem to have sent to Massachusetts; so it is quite likely that the men who fought at Bunker Hill may have loaded their guns with some of the powder given them by their friends in Savannah. In that case, the king got his powder back, but in a somewhat different way from what he expected!

---

4   Silkworm: a kind of caterpillar that spins a fine, soft thread of which silk is made.

General Oglethorpe spent the end of his life in England. He lived to a very old age. Up to the last, they say, he had eyes as bright and sharp as a boy's. After the Revolution was over, the king made a treaty in which he promised to let the United States of America live in peace. General Oglethorpe was able to read that treaty without spectacles. He had lived to see the colony of Georgia become a free and independent state within the Union.

## Summary

In 1733 General James Oglethorpe brought over a number of emigrants from England. They then settled Savannah, Georgia. Georgia was the 13th English colony; it was the last one established in this country. General Oglethorpe lived to see it become one of the United States of America.

## Questions

At the beginning of 1733, before Georgia was founded, how many English colonies were there in America?

Who was General Oglethorpe?

What did he do?

Why was the new settlement called Georgia?

What happened to a friend of General Oglethorpe's that inspired him to create Georgia?

What did he plan to do for the poor debtors?

What do you know about the settlement of Savannah?

What about the German emigrants and Ebenezer?

Was it a good idea to raise silk in Georgia? Why or why not?

Why were the citizens of the Carolinas happy the newcomers were living in Georgia?

What does it mean that "the king got his powder back, but in a somewhat different way from what he expected!?"

What happened to General Oglethorpe in his old age?

# Benjamin Franklin
### 1706-1790

## Growth of Philadelphia; what a young printer was doing for it

By the mid-1700s, Philadelphia had surpassed Boston as the largest city in British America. In fact, it was the second largest city in all the British Empire.

Next to William Penn, the person who did the most for Philadelphia was a young man who had left Boston to make his home among the Quakers. He lived in a small

Franklin printing his newspaper

house near the market. On a board over the door he had painted his name and business; here it is:

## Franklin's newspaper and almanac; how he worked; standing before kings

Already in 1729, Ben Franklin was publishing a small newspaper called the Pennsylvania Gazette. Today, the fastest printing presses can produce 90,000 copies of a 96-page newspaper in an hour. But Franklin, standing in his shirtsleeves at a little press, printed his little two-page newspaper with his own hands. It was hard work, as you could see by the drops of sweat that stood on his forehead. And it was slow as well as hard.

The young man not only wrote most of what he printed in his paper, but he often made his own ink. Sometimes he even made his own type.[1] When he ran out of paper, he would take a wheelbarrow, go out and buy a load, and wheel it home. Today there are more than a dozen major newspapers printed in Philadelphia. At that time, there were only two. And Franklin's was the better of those two.

Franklin wheeling a load of paper.

A piece of type.

The letter B.

Besides the Gazette, he published an almanac which thousands of people bought. In it he printed such sayings as these: "*He who would thrive[2] must rise at five,*" and "*If you want a thing well done, do it yourself.*" But Franklin was not contented with simply printing these sayings. He practiced them as well.

---

1 Type: small blocks of metal or wood that bear raised letters or characters on one end. These raised forms leave printed impressions when inked and pressed on paper. Until the mid-1900s, type was made by melting lead and other metals together and pouring the mixture into molds.
2 Thrive: to get on in business, to prosper.

Sometimes his friends would ask him why he began work so early in the morning and kept at it so many hours. He would laugh, and tell them that his father used to repeat to him this saying of Solomon: *"Seest thou a man diligent in his business? he shall stand before kings; he shall not stand before mean[3] men."*[4]

At that time the young printer never actually expected to stand in the presence of a king, but years later he met with five kings; and one of them, his friend the king of France, gave him his picture set round with diamonds.

## Franklin's boyhood; making tallow candles; he is apprenticed[5] to his brother; how he managed to save money to buy books

Franklin's father was a poor man with a large family. He lived in Boston, and made soap and candles. Benjamin went to school for two years. Then, when he was ten years old, his father set him to work in his factory, and he never went to school again. He was now kept busy filling the candle-molds with melted grease, cutting off the ends of the wicks, and running errands. But the boy did not like this kind of work; and, as he was very fond of books, his father put him in a printing office. This office was run by James Franklin, one of Ben's older brothers.

James Franklin paid a small sum of money each week for Ben's board; but the boy told him that if he would let him have half the money to use as he liked, he would board him-

---

3 Mean: poor, lowly, of inferior quality. It does not mean hurtful, though a mean person may be hurtful.

4 See Proverbs 22:29 in the Bible.

5 Apprenticed: bound by a written agreement to learn a trade from a skilled master. The same agreement binds the master to teach the trade. The person who is apprenticed is called an apprentice.

self. James was glad to do this. Benjamin then gave up eating meat, and, while the others went out to dinner, he would stay in the printing-office and eat a boiled potato, or perhaps a handful of raisins. In this way, he saved up a number of copper coins every week; and when he got enough laid by, he would buy a book.

But James Franklin was not only a mean man, but a hot-tempered one; and when he got angry with his young apprentice, he would beat him. At length, Benjamin, who was now 17, made up his mind to run away and go to New York.

## Young Franklin runs away; he goes to New York, and then to Philadelphia

Map 22. Benjamin Franklin's American travels.

Young Franklin sold some of his books and used the money to pay his passage to New York. In those days there were no railroads or ships with engines. So he took a sailboat. When he got to New York, he could find no work, so he decided to go on to Philadelphia.

He started to walk across New Jersey to Burlington, on the Delaware River, a distance of about fifty miles. There he hoped to get a sailboat going down the river to Philadelphia. Shortly after he set out, it began to rain hard, and Ben was soon wet to the skin and covered with red mud. He kept on until noon, took a rest, and on the third day reached Burlington where he got passage down the river.

## Franklin's Sunday walk in Philadelphia; the rolls; Miss Read; the Quaker meeting house

Franklin landed in Philadelphia on a Sunday morning in 1723. He was tired and hungry. He had but a single dollar in the world. As he walked along, he saw a bakeshop open. He went in and bought three great, puffy rolls for a penny[6] each. Then he started up Market Street.

Franklin's first day in Philadelphia.

He had a roll like a small loaf of bread tucked under each arm, and he was eating the other as though it tasted good to him. As he passed a house, he noticed a nice looking young woman at the door. She seemed to want to laugh and it is possible she did laugh, since Franklin looked as if he were a youthful tramp who had robbed a baker's shop. The young woman was Miss Deborah Read. A number of years later Franklin married her. He always said that he could not have found a better wife.

---

6 Penny: at the time, a penny was an English coin that was worth two cents compared to the American penny that would be produced many years later.

Franklin kept on in his walk until he came to the Delaware. He took a hearty drink of river water to settle his breakfast, then gave away the two rolls he had under his arm to a poor woman with a child. On his way back from the river he followed a number of people to a Quaker meeting house. At the meeting, no one spoke. Franklin was tired out,

Stoop! Stoop!

and, not having any preacher to keep him awake, he soon fell asleep, and slept till the meeting was over. He says, "This was the first house I was in, or slept in, in Philadelphia."

## Franklin finds work; he goes back to Boston on a visit; he learns to stoop

The next day the young man found some work in a printing office. Six months afterward he decided to go back to Boston to see his friends. He started on his journey with a good suit of clothes, a silver watch, and a well-filled purse.

While in Boston, Franklin went to call on a minister who had written a little book that he had grown very fond of reading.[7]

As he was coming away from the minister's house, he had to go through a low passageway under a large beam. "Stoop! Stoop!" cried the gentleman; but Franklin did not understand him, and so hit his head a sharp knock against the beam.

---

7  The name of the book: *Essays to do Good* by the Rev. Cotton Mather.

"Ah," said his friend, as he saw him rubbing his head, "you are young, and have the world before you; stoop as you go through it, and you will miss many hard thumps." Franklin says that this sensible advice, which was thus beat into his head, was of great use afterward. In fact, he learned then how to stoop to conquer.

## Franklin returns to Philadelphia; he goes to London; water against beer

Franklin soon went back to Philadelphia. The governor of Pennsylvania then persuaded him to go to London. He told Franklin that he would help him get a printing press and type to start a newspaper in Philadelphia.

When Franklin reached London, he found that the governor was one of those men who promise great things but do nothing. Instead of buying a press, he had to go to work in a printing office to earn his bread. He stayed in London for more than a year. At the office where he worked, the men were great beer drinkers. One of his companions bought six pints a day. He began with a pint before breakfast, then took another pint at breakfast, a pint between breakfast and dinner ("lunch"), a pint at dinner, a pint in the afternoon, and, last of all, a pint after he had done work. Franklin drank nothing but water. The others laughed at him, and nicknamed him the "Water-American"; but after a while they had to confess that he was stronger than they were who drank so much strong beer.

The fact was that Franklin could beat them both at work and at play. When they went out for a bath in the Thames,[8] they found that their "Water-American" could swim like a

---

8　Thames (Temz). London is on the river Thames.

fish. Indeed, he so astonished them that a rich Londoner tried to persuade him to start a swimming school to teach his sons. But Franklin had stayed in England long enough, and he decided to go back to Philadelphia.

## Franklin sets up his newspaper; "sawdust pudding"

After his return to America, Franklin labored so diligently that he was soon able to set up a newspaper of his own. He tried to make it a good one. But some people thought that he spoke his mind too freely. They complained of this to him, and let him know that if he did not make his paper to please them, they would stop taking it or advertising in it.

Franklin heard what they had to say, and then invited them all to come and have supper with him. They went. They expected a feast but found nothing on the table beside two dishes of corn-meal mush and a big pitcher of cold water. At that time, mush was eaten only by very poor people; and because it was yellow and coarse, people called it "sawdust pudding."

Franklin gave everybody a heaping plateful, and then, filling his own, he made a hearty supper of it. The others tried to eat, but couldn't. After Franklin had finished his supper, he looked up, and said quietly, "My friends, anyone who can live on 'sawdust pudding' and cold water, as I can, does not need much help from others." After that, no one went to the young printer with complaints about his paper. Franklin, as we have seen, had learned to stoop; but he certainly did not mean to go stooping through life.

## Franklin's plan of life; what he did for Philadelphia

Not many young men can see their own faults, but Franklin could. More than that, he tried hard to get rid of them. Indeed, he set a plan to pursue and, if possible, to arrive at moral perfection. He kept a little book in which he studied 13 virtues[9] that he would attempt to master. At the end of each day, he wrote down any of his failings. If he wasted half an hour of time or a shilling of money, or said anything that would have been better not said, he wrote it down in his book. He carried that book in his pocket all his life, and he studied it the way a good student studies a hard lesson.

As a result of this discipline, Franklin learned three things: first, to do the right thing; next, to do it at the right time; and last, to do it in the right way.

As he was never tired of helping himself to get upward and onward, so, too, Franklin never tired of helping others. He started the first lending library in Philadelphia, which, as it turns out, was also the first such library in America. He created the first fire company ("fire department") and the first military company (to provide defense against invasion) in that city. He got the people to pave the muddy streets with stone. He helped to build the first academy, now called the University of Pennsylvania. And he also helped to build the first hospital.

---

9   Virtues: qualities considered morally good or desirable.

## Franklin's experiments[10] with electricity; the wonderful bottle; the picture of the king of England

While doing these things and publishing his paper besides, Franklin found time to make experiments with electricity. Very little was then known about electricity. But a Dutchman had discovered a way of bottling it up. The man lived in the city of Leyden[11] in Holland, so his device became known as a Leyden Jar. Franklin had one of these jars, and he never grew tired of seeing what new and strange thing he could do with it.

He created a picture of the king of England with a movable gold crown on his head. Then he connected the crown, by a long wire, to the Leyden Jar. When he wanted some fun, he would dare any one to go up to the picture and take off the king's crown. Why, that's easy enough, a man would say. And he would walk up and seize the crown. But no sooner had he touched it than he would get an electric shock that made his fingers tingle like they had never tingled before. With a loud Oh! Oh! he would let go of the crown, and start back in utter astonishment, having no idea what had hurt him.

## The electrical kite

But Franklin's greatest experiment was made one day in all seriousness—with a kite. He believed that the electricity in the bottle, or Leyden Jar, was the same thing as the lightning we see in a thunderstorm. He knew well enough how to get an electric spark from the jar. Indeed, he had once killed a turkey with it for dinner. But how could he get a spark from a cloud in the sky?

---

10 Experiments: here an experiment is a trial made to discover something unknown. Franklin made these experiments or trials with electricity and with thunder clouds in order to find out what he could about them.

11 Leyden: see Map 12, p. 50.

He thought about it for a long time. Then he made a kite out of a silk handkerchief, and fastened a sharp iron point to the upright stick of the kite. One day, when he saw a thunderstorm coming, Franklin and his son went out to the fields. They flew the kite and tied an iron key to the lower end of the string. After waiting some time, Franklin saw the little hair-like threads of the string begin to stand up like the bristles of a brush. He was sure that the electricity was coming down the string. He put his knuckle close to the key, and a spark flew out. Next, he took his Leyden Jar and collected the electricity in that.[12] He had made two great discoveries, for he had found out that electricity and lightning are the same thing, and he had also found how to fill his bottle directly from the clouds. That was something that no one had ever done before.

---

12 WARNING: Do not try Franklin's experiment yourself! In fact, it is astonishing that Franklin wasn't killed by the lightning. After Franklin did his experiment, several other experimenters tried the same thing and were electrocuted by the lightning.

## Franklin invents the lightning rod; *Doctor* Franklin

But Franklin did not stop at the kite string experiment. He said, "If I can draw down electricity from the sky with a kite-string, I can draw it still better with a tall, sharp-pointed iron rod. And if I attach that rod to a metal wire that goes to the ground, perhaps I can stop houses from catching on fire when they are struck by lightning."

He put up such a rod on his house in Philadelphia; it was the first lightning rod in the world. Soon other people began to put them up. So this was another gift of his to the city he loved. Every good lightning rod that has since been erected to protect buildings is a copy of the rod invented by Franklin.

People now began to talk, not only in America but in Europe, about his electrical experiments and discoveries. The University of St. Andrews, the oldest college in Scotland, gave him a title of honor. They called him Doctor—a word that means a learned man. From that time on, Franklin the printer was no longer plain Mr. Franklin, but Dr. Franklin.

Dr. Franklin did not think that he had found all that could be found about electricity; he believed that he had simply made a beginning, and that others would discover still greater things that could be done with it. Do you think he was mistaken about that?

## Franklin in the Revolutionary War; Franklin and the map of the United States

When the American Revolutionary war broke out, Dr. Franklin did a great work for his country. He did not fight battles like General Washington, but he did something just as useful.

First, he helped write the Declaration of Independence, by which the United States of America declared themselves free from the rule of the king of England. Next, he went to France to get aid for the states. At the time, the American states were too poor to pay their soldiers. Franklin got the king of France to let them have money to pay the soldiers.

Franklin lived to see the Revolution end and the American states acquire their independence from Britain. When he died, full of years and of honors, he was buried in Philadelphia. Twenty thousand people went to his funeral.

Franklin's cane and Washington's Revolutionary sword.

Preserved in the Patent Office, Washington.

If you want to see what the country thinks of him, you have only to look at a large map of the United States, and count up how many times you find his name on it. You will find that there are almost 200 towns, cities, counties and townships in the United States with the name Franklin in them.

## Summary

Benjamin Franklin was born in Boston over 300 years ago. He went to Philadelphia when he was 17. He started a newspaper there, opened the first public library, and did many other things to help the city. He discovered that lightning and electricity are the same thing, and he invented the lightning rod to protect buildings. In the Revolution, he got large sums of

Franklin's grave in Christ Church burial ground, Philadelphia.

money from the king of France to pay American soldiers to help Washington fight the battles that ended in the America colonies becoming independent from Britain.

## Questions

What had Philadelphia grown to be by the mid-1700s?

Who did a great deal for Philadelphia?

Tell what you can about Franklin's newspaper, the *Philadelphia Gazette*.

What else did he publish?

What kinds of sayings did he print in his almanac?

Franklin's father used to repeat to him a saying from Solomon about being diligent in one's work. According to the saying, what is the reward for diligence and the punishment for slacking off?

Did Franklin ever stand in the presence of any kings?

Tell what you can about Franklin as a boy.

Where did he live?

What did he do?

How did he save money to buy books?

Why did he run away from his brother?

Where did he go?

Tell what you can about Franklin's landing in Philadelphia.

How did Franklin look to Miss Read?

Where did Franklin find work?

What happened to him when he visited the Rev. Mather when he went to Boston on a visit?

What does it mean that Franklin learned to "stoop to conquer"?

The governor of Pennsylvania sent Franklin to London. What did he say he wanted to help Franklin do in London?

What did Franklin wind up doing in London?

Franklin's fellow workers in London gave him a nickname that was meant to embarrass him. What was the name and why did they give it to him?

Was it a good name for Franklin? Why or why not?

What did Franklin do after he returned to Philadelphia?

Tell the story of the "sawdust pudding."

Tell about Franklin's plan of life and the little book he kept to help him follow it.

What did Franklin do for Philadelphia?

What experiments did Franklin make?

What about the picture of the king?

Tell the story of the kite.

What two things did Franklin find out by means of his kite?

Franklin invented many things, but which invention does this book talk about?

What title did the University of St. Andrews in Scotland give him?

Did Franklin think that anything more would be discovered about electricity?

What two things did Franklin do in the American Revolution?

What is said of his funeral?

About how many towns, cities, counties and townships in the United States are now called by his name?

"Yankee Doodle" or The Spirit of '76.

# George Washington

1732-1799

Stone that marks Washington's birthplace. The house disappeared long ago.

### A Virginia boy; what he became; what he learned at school; his writing books

In 1732, when Franklin was at work on his newspaper, a boy was born on a plantation (or large estate cultivated by slaves) on Bridges Creek, a small stream that emptied into the Potomac River.[1] The baby was one day to stand higher, even, than the Philadelphia printer.

That boy, when he grew up, was to be chosen leader of the armies of the Revolution; he was to be elected the first president of the United States; and, before he died, he was to be known and honored all over the world. The name of that boy was George Washington.

*March 12th 1744/5*

*Geo Washington*

Washington's signature at the age of 12.

---

1 Not long after he was born, George's family moved to an estate on the Rappahannock River, opposite Fredericksburg. See Map 23, p. 120 for both of these places—where Washington was born and the family's estate.

Washington's father died when George was only 11 years old. This left George and his brothers and sisters in the care of a most excellent and sensible mother. It was this mother's influence, more than anything else, that made George the man he became.

George went to a little country school, where he learned to read, write, and do arithmetic. By the time he was twelve, George could write with clear, bold letters. In one of his writing-books he copied many good rules or sayings. Here is one:

Labor to keep alive in your breast
that little spark of celestial[2] fire
called conscience.

## Washington's sports and games; playing at war; "Captain George"

Young Washington was not always copying good sayings. He was a tall, strong boy, fond of all outdoor sports and games. He was a well-meaning boy, but he had a hot temper, and at times his blue eyes flashed fire. In all trials of strength and in all deeds of daring, George took the lead. He could run faster, jump further, and throw a stone higher than anyone else in his school.

When the boys played "soldier," they liked to have "Captain George" as commander. When he drew his wooden sword and shouted "Come on!" they would all rush into battle with a wild hurrah. Years afterward, when real wars came and George Washington drew his sword in earnest, some of his school companions may have fought under their old leader.

---

2 Celestial: heavenly, divine.

## The great battle with the colt, and what came of it

Once, Washington had a different kind of battle. It was with a high-spirited colt that belonged to his mother. Nobody had ever been able to do anything with that colt, and most people were afraid of him.

Early one morning, George and some of his brothers were out in the pasture. George looked at the colt prancing about and kicking up his heels. Then he said: "Boys, if you'll help me put a bridle on him, I'll ride him." The boys managed to get the colt into a corner and to slip on the bridle. With a leap, George seated himself firmly on his back. Then the fun began. The colt, wild with rage, ran, jumped, plunged, and reared straight up on his hind legs, hoping to throw his rider off. It was all useless. He might as well have tried to throw off his own skin, for George stuck to his back as though he had grown there. Then, making a last desperate bound into the air, the animal burst a blood-vessel and fell dead. The battle was over, George was victor, but it had cost the life of Mrs. Washington's favorite colt.

When the boys went in to breakfast, their mother, knowing that they had just come from the pasture, asked how the colt was getting on. "He is dead, madam," said George; "I killed him."

"Dead!" exclaimed his mother.

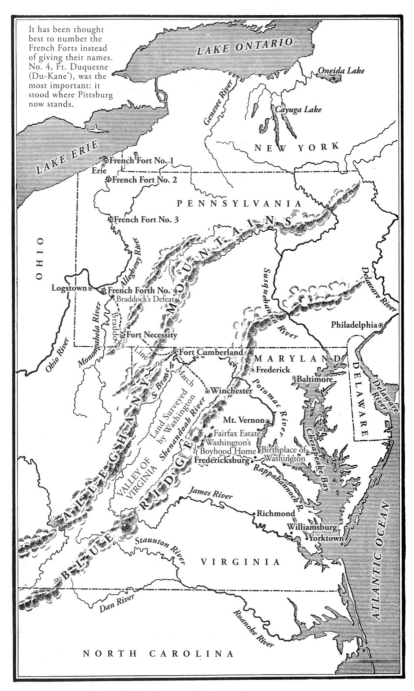

It has been thought best to number the French Forts instead of giving their names. No. 4, Ft. Duquesne (Du-Kane'), was the most important: it stood where Pittsburg now stands.

Map 23. The land George Washington knew as a young man.

"Yes, madam, dead," replied her son. Then he told her just how it happened. When Mrs. Washington heard the story, her face flushed with anger. Then, waiting a moment, she looked steadily at George, and said quietly, "While I regret the loss of my favorite, I rejoice in my son, who always speaks the truth."

## Washington goes on a visit to Mount Vernon; he makes the acquaintance of Lord Fairfax

George's eldest brother, Lawrence, had married the daughter of a gentleman named Fairfax,[3] who lived on the banks of the Potomac. Lawrence had a fine estate a few miles above Fairfax on the same river. He called his place Mount Vernon. When he was 14, George went to Mount Vernon to visit his brother.

Lawrence Washington took George down the river to call on the Fairfaxes. There the boy made the acquaintance of Lord Fairfax, an English nobleman who had come over from London. He owned an immense piece of land in Virginia. Lord Fairfax and George soon became great friends. He was a gray haired man of nearly 60. But he enjoyed having this boy of 14 as a companion. They spent weeks together on horse-back in the fields and woods, hunting deer and foxes.

## Lord Fairfax hires Washington to survey[4] his land; how Washington lived in the woods

Lord Fairfax's land extended westward more than 100 miles. It had never been very carefully surveyed; and he was told

---

3 Fairfax. This was William Fairfax, cousin to Lord Fairfax. William had the responsibility of caring for Lord Fairfax's land.

4 Survey: to find out the form, size, and position of a piece of land by measuring it in certain ways.

that settlers were moving in beyond the Blue Ridge Mountains.[5] They were building log-cabins on his property without asking permission. By the time Washington was 16, he had learned a few things about surveying; and so Lord Fairfax hired him to measure his land for him. Washington was glad to undertake

Washington sees an Indian war-dance.

the work. He needed money, and he could earn £4 to £6 a day—easily 20 times as much as the average school teacher— by serving Lord Fairfax in this way.

Early in the spring, Washington, in company with another young man, started off on foot to do this business. They crossed the Blue Ridge Mountains, and entered the Valley of Virginia, one of the most beautiful valleys in America.

The two young men would work all day in the woods with a long chain, measuring the land. When evening came, Washington would make a map of what they had measured. Then they would wrap themselves up in their blankets, stretch

5   Blue Ridge Mountains: See Map 23, p. 120.

themselves on the ground at the foot of a tree, and go to sleep under the stars.

Every day they shot some game—squirrels or wild turkeys, or perhaps a deer. They kindled a fire with flint and steel, and roasted the meat on sticks held over the coals. For plates they used clean chips of wood. And since clean chips could always be had by a few blows of an axe, they never washed any dishes, but just threw them away, and created a new set for each meal.

When Washington returned from his surveying trip, Lord Fairfax was greatly pleased with his work; and the governor of Virginia made him one of the public surveyors. By this means he was able to get work that paid him handsomely.

**Washington at the age of 21; the French in the west; the governor of Virginia sends Washington to see the French commander**

By the time Washington was 21, he had grown to be over six feet tall. He was straight as an arrow and tough as a whiplash. He had keen blue eyes that seemed to look into the very heart of things, and his fist was like a blacksmith's sledgehammer. He knew all about the woods, all about Indians, and he could take care of himself anywhere.

At this time, the English settlers held the country along the seashore as far back as the Allegheny Mountains.[6] West of those mountains, the French from Canada were trying to get possession of the land. They had made friends with many of the Indians, and they hoped, with the Indians' help, to be able to drive out the English and get the whole country for themselves.

---

6   Allegheny (Al'leh-gay'nee): see Map 23, p. 120. (It is also spelled Alleghany.)

In order to hold this land in the west, the French had built several forts south of Lake Erie, and they were getting ready to build some on the Ohio River. The governor of Virginia was determined to put a stop to this. He had given young Washington the military title of major;[7] he now sent Major Washington to see the French commander at one of the forts near Lake Erie. Washington was to tell the Frenchman that he had built his forts on land belonging to the English, and that he and his men must either leave or fight.

Major Washington dressed himself like an Indian and, attended by several friendly Indians and by an English settler who knew the country well, he set out on his journey through what was called the Great Woods.

The entire distance to the farthest fort and back was about 1,000 miles. Washington could go on horseback part of the way, but there were no regular roads, and he had to climb mountains and swim rivers. After several weeks' travel, he reached the fort, but the French commander refused to give up the land. He said that he and his men had come to stay, and that if the English did not like it, they must fight.

### The journey back; the Indian guide; how Washington found his way through the woods; the adventure with the raft

On the way back, Washington had to leave his horses and come on foot with his English companion and an Indian guide sent from the fort. This Indian guide was in the pay of the French, and he intended to murder Washington in the woods.

---

7   Major (ma'jer): an officer in the army next above a captain but below a colonel.

One day, the Indian shot at Washington from behind a tree. He did not hit Washington. At that point, Washington and his settler companion managed to get away from the Indian, and set out to go back to Virginia by themselves.

There were no paths through the thick forest; but Washington had his compass with him, and with that he could find his way just as the captain of a ship finds his way at sea. When they reached the Allegheny River they found it full of floating ice. They worked all day and made a raft of logs. As they were pushing their way across with poles, a big piece of ice struck Washington's pole which, he said, jerked him out into water ten feet deep.

At length, the two men managed to get to a little island, but as there was no wood on it, they could not make a fire. The weather was bitterly cold, and Washington, who was soaked to the skin, had to take his choice between walking about all night, or trying to sleep on the frozen ground in his wet clothes.

## Major Washington becomes Colonel Washington; Fort Necessity; Braddock's defeat

When Major Washington got back to Virginia, the governor made him colonel. And the governor then ordered Colonel Washington to set out for the west with 150 men. He was told to "make prisoners, kill or destroy" all Frenchmen who might try to take possession of land on the Ohio River.

Washington built a small log fort that he named Fort Necessity.[8] The French attacked his troop there. They had five men to every one of his. Colonel Washington fought like a

---

8   Fort Necessity: see Map 23, p. 120.

General Braddock's fall on the battlefield.

man who liked to hear the bullets whistle past his ears,—as he said he did,—but in the end he had to give up the fort.

Then General Braddock, a noted English soldier, was sent over to Virginia by the king of England to drive the French out of the country. Braddock started with a fine army, and Washington went with him.[9] Washington told Braddock that the French and the Indians would hide in the woods and fire at his men from behind trees. But Braddock paid no attention to the warning. On his way through the forest, the brave English general was suddenly struck down by the enemy, half of his army was killed or wounded, and the rest of the men were put to flight. Washington had two horses

9   See "Braddock's Line of March," Map 23, p. 120.

shot out from under him, and four bullets went through his coat. It was a narrow escape for the young man. One of those who fought in the battle said, "I expected every moment to see him fall"—but Washington was to live for greater work.

## End of the war with the French; what the king of England wanted to do; how the American people felt toward him

The war with the French lasted a number of years. It ended by the English getting possession of the whole of America from the Atlantic Ocean to the Mississippi River. All this part of America was ruled by George III, King of England. The king now determined to send over more soldiers, and to keep them in his American colonies to prevent the French in Canada from trying to get back the country they had lost. He wanted the people in his colonies to pay the cost of keeping these soldiers. But the people were not willing to do this because they felt they were able to protect themselves without help of any kind.

At this, the king said, "If the Americans will not give the money, then I will take it from them by force—for pay it they must and shall." This was more than the king would have dared say about the people in England; for there, if he wanted money to spend on his army, he had to ask Parliament for the privilege, and Parliament could agree to give it or not, as they thought best.

The Americans said, "We have the same rights as our brothers in England, and the king cannot force us to give a single copper against our will. If he tries to take it from us, we will fight. Some of the greatest men in England agreed with us, and said that they would fight, too, if they were in our place."

The Boston "Tea Party."

## The king determines to have the money; the tea-ships, and the "Boston tea-party"

George III did not know the Americans, and he did not think that they meant what they said. He tried to make them pay the money he needed to keep his soldiers in the colonies. But the American colonists refused. From Maine to Georgia, only a few people were willing to obey the king.

Then the king thought that he would try a different method. Shiploads of tea were sent over to New York, Boston, Philadelphia, and Charleston. If the tea should be landed and sold, then every man who bought a pound of it would have to pay six cents more than the regular price. That six cents was a tax, and it went into the British government's pocket.

The majority of Americans said, "We won't pay those six cents!"

When the tea reached New York, the citizens sent it back again to England. They did the same thing at Philadelphia. At Charleston they let it be brought onshore, but they stored it in damp cellars. People would not buy any of it any more than they would buy so much poison ... so it all rotted and spoiled.

At Boston, they had a grand "tea party." A number of men dressed themselves up like Indians, went on board the tea ships at night, broke open all the chests, and emptied the tea into the harbor.

## The king closes the port of Boston; Congress meets at Philadelphia; the names American and British; what General Gage tried to do

The king was terribly angry. He had his prime minister order that the port of Boston should be closed, so that no ships, except the king's warships, should come in or go out.

Nearly all trade stopped in Boston. Many of the inhabitants began to suffer for want of food, but throughout the colonies the people tried their best to help them.

The New England towns sent droves of sheep and cattle. New York sent wheat. South Carolina gave two hundred barrels of rice. The other colonies gave liberally in money and provisions. Even in England, many leaders expressed sympathy for the distressed people of Boston, and in London a large sum of money was raised to help those whom the king was determined to starve into submission.

The colonies now sent some of their best men to Philadelphia to consider what should be done. As this meeting was made up of those who had come from all parts of the country, it took the name of the General, or Continental, Congress.

Map 24. The Northern states in the American Revolution.

About this time, too, a great change took place. The people throughout the country began to call themselves Americans. And they began to speak of the English troops as British soldiers.

In Boston, General Gage had command of these British soldiers. He knew that the Americans were getting ready to fight, and that they had stored up powder and ball at Concord, about 20 miles from Boston. One night, he secretly sent soldiers to march to Concord and destroy the colonists' military supplies.

## Paul Revere; the fight at Lexington and Concord; Bunker Hill

Paul Revere, a Boston man, was on the watch; and as soon as he found out which way the British were going, he set off at a gallop for Lexington, on the road to Concord. All the way out, he roused people from their sleep, with the cry, "The British are coming!"

When the king's soldiers reached Lexington, they found the Americans, under Captain Parker, ready for them. Captain Parker said to his men, "Don't fire unless you are fired on. But if they want a war, let it begin here." The fighting did begin there, April 19th, 1775. And when the British left the town on their way to Concord, seven Americans lay dead on the grass in front of the village church. At Concord, that same day, there was still harder fighting; and on the way back to Boston, a large number of the British were killed.

The next month, June 17th, 1775, a battle was fought on Bunker Hill in Charlestown, just outside of Boston. General Gage thought the Americans—"Yankees"—wouldn't fight. But they did fight, in a way that General Gage never

Paul Revere's Ride.

forgot. And though the Yankees' powder ran out so they had to retreat, the British lost more than a thousand men in the battle.

The contest at Bunker Hill was the first great battle of the Revolution—the war that overturned the British power in America. Many Englishmen thought the king was wrong. They would not fight against the Americans, and he was obliged to hire a large number of German soldiers to send to America. These Germans had to fight whether they wanted to or not, because their king forced them to fight.

## Colonel Washington at Mount Vernon; Congress makes him General Washington, and sends him to take command of the American army

At the time the battle of Bunker Hill was fought, Colonel George Washington was living very quietly in Mount

Washington at Mount Vernon overseeing his black slaves.

Washington takes command of the American army at Cambridge.

Vernon. His brother Lawrence had died, and Mount Vernon was now his home. Washington was very wealthy. He had a fine estate and plenty of slaves to do the work on it.[10]

Congress now made Colonel Washington general, and sent him to Cambridge, a town just outside of Boston, to take command of the American army. It was called the Continental Army because it was raised, not to fight for the people of Massachusetts, but for all the American colonies on the continent. Washington took command of the army on July 3, 1775. He stood under a great elm on the Cambridge Common in Massachusetts. There, six months later, he raised the first American flag.[11]

---

10 Washington's slaves: Washington freed none of his slaves while he lived. In his will, however, he left orders that all of his slaves should be set free as soon as it could be done.
11 See a picture of this and the other flags of the Revolution on p. 144.

"Now, General Gage, look out for *your* nose!"

## American sharpshooters;[12] Washington's need of cannon and powder; the attack on Canada; the British driven out of Boston

Men now came from all parts of the country to join the Continental Army. Many of them were sharpshooters. In one case an officer set up a board with the figure of a man's nose chalked on it as a target. A hundred men fired at it at long distance. Sixty hit the nose. The newspapers gave them great praise for their skill and said, "Now, General Gage, look out for *your* nose."

Washington wanted to drive General Gage and the British soldiers out of Boston, but for months he could not get either cannon or powder. Benjamin Franklin said that the Americans would have to fight as the Indians used to, with bows and arrows.

---

12 Sharpshooters: men who can fire and hit a small mark with a bullet at a long distance.

While Washington was waiting, a number of Americans marched against the British in Canada; but the cold weather came on, and they nearly starved to death. Some of the men were so hungry, they took off their moccasins[13] and gnawed them, while they danced in the snow to keep their bare feet from freezing.

At last, Washington got both cannon and powder. He dragged the cannon up to the top of some high land overlooking Boston harbor. He then sent word to General Howe (since Gage had gone) that, if he did not leave Boston, he would knock Howe's ships to pieces. The British saw that they could not help themselves, so they made haste to get on board their vessels and sail away. They never came back to Boston again. But they went to New York.

"Down with the King!"

### The Declaration of Independence; "Down with the king!"; Washington is driven from New York and across the Delaware River

Washington got to New York first.

---

13 Moccasins (mok'uh-sins): Indian shoes made of deerskin.

While he was there, on the 4th of July, 1776, Congress declared the United States were independent—that is, entirely free from the rule of the king of England.

There was a gilded[14] lead statue of King George III on horseback in New York City. When the news of what Congress had done reached that city, there was a great cry of "Down with the king!" That night, some men pulled down the statue, melted it up, and cast it into bullets.

The next month there was a battle on Long Island,[15] just across from New York City. The British gained the victory. Washington had to leave New York, and Lord Cornwallis, one of the British generals, chased him and his little army clear across the State of New Jersey. It looked at one time as though all the Americans would be taken prisoner, but Washington managed to seize a lot of small boats on the Delaware River[15] and get across into Pennsylvania. Since the British had no boats, they could not follow.

## Washington's victory at Trenton, New Jersey

Lord Cornwallis left 1500 German soldiers at Trenton on the Delaware. He intended, as soon as the river froze, to cross on the ice and attack Washington's army. But Washington did not wait for him. On Christmas night (1776) he took a large number of boats, filled them with soldiers, and secretly crossed over to New Jersey.[16] The weather was intensely cold, the river was full of floating ice, and a furious snowstorm set in. Many of the American soldiers had nothing more than rags to wear and had only old broken shoes. They suffered terribly, and two of them froze to death.

---

14 Gilded: gold-covered.
15 Long Island; Delaware River: See Map 24, p. 130.
16 New Jersey: See Map 24, p. 130.

The Germans at Trenton had been having a jolly Christmas, and had gone to bed. They expected no danger. Suddenly, Washington and his men rushed into the little town and, almost before they knew what had happened, a thousand Germans were made prisoners. The rest escaped to tell Lord Cornwallis how the Americans had beaten them. When Washington was driven out of New York, many Americans thought he would be captured. But now they were filled with joy. The battle of Trenton was the first battle of the war that was won by the Continental Army.

## The American victory at Princeton, New Jersey; the British take Philadelphia; winter at Valley Forge; Burgoyne[17] beaten; the king of France agrees to help the Americans

Washington took his thousand prisoners over into Pennsylvania. A few days later, he again crossed the Delaware into

Valley Forge.

17 Burgoyne (Ber'goyn).

New Jersey. While Cornwallis was fast asleep in his tent, Washington slipped round him, got to Princeton,[18] and again beat a part of the British army.

Cornwallis woke up and heard Washington's cannon. "That's thunder," he said. He was right; it was the thunder of another American victory.

Before the next winter set in, however, the British had taken the city of Philadelphia which was, at that time, the capital of the United States. Meanwhile, through the winter of 1777-78, Washington's army froze and starved on the hillsides of Valley Forge,[18] about 20 miles northwest of Philadelphia.

But good news was coming. The Americans had won a great victory over the British General Burgoyne at Saratoga, New York,[18] in late September and early October of 1777. Dr. Franklin was in Paris. When he heard that Burgoyne had been beaten, he hurried off to the palace of the French king to tell him about it. The king of France hated the British, and he agreed to send money, ships, and soldiers to help the Americans. When the men at Valley Forge heard the news, they leaped and hurrahed for joy. Not long after that, the British left Philadelphia, and American troops entered in triumph.

## The war at the South; Jasper; Cowpens; Greene and Cornwallis

While these things were happening in the north, the British sent a fleet of vessels to take Charleston, South Carolina.[19] They hammered away with their big guns at a little log fort under command of Colonel Moultrie. During the battle, a

---

18  Princeton; Valley Forge; Saratoga, New York: See Map 24, p. 130.
19  Charleston, South Carolina: See Map 25, p. 141.

cannonball struck the flagpole on the fort, and cut it in two. The South Carolina flag fell to the ground outside the fort. Sergeant[20] William Jasper leaped down, and, while British shot was striking all around him, he seized the flag, climbed back, fastened it to a short staff, and raised it to its place, to show that the Americans would never give up the fort. After fighting all day, the British saw that they could do nothing against palmetto logs[21] when defended by such men as Moultrie and Jasper; so they sailed away with those of their ships that had not been destroyed.

Several years later, the British did take Charleston. Lord Cornwallis then took command of the British army in South Carolina. General Greene of Rhode Island commanded

Sergeant Jasper and the flag.

---

20  Sergeant (sar'jent): a military officer of low rank.
21  Palmetto logs: the wood of the palmetto tree is very soft and spongy; the cannon-balls, when they struck, would bury themselves in the logs, but would neither break them to pieces nor go through them.

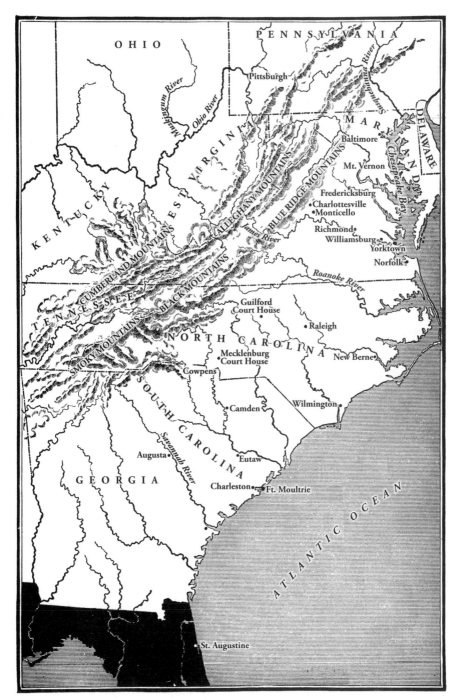

Map 25. The Southern states in the American Revolution.

the Americans. Greene sent Daniel Morgan with his sharp-shooters to meet part of the British army at Cowpens;[22] they did meet them, and sent them flying. Then Cornwallis determined to either whip Greene or drive him out of the state. But Greene harassed Cornwallis so much that Cornwallis was eventually glad to get out of the Carolinas and escape into Virginia. He had found North and South Carolina like two hornets' nests, and the further he got away from those hornets, the better he liked it.

## Cornwallis and Benedict Arnold; Lafayette; Cornwallis traps himself in Yorktown

Lafayette

When Lord Cornwallis got into Virginia, he found Benedict Arnold waiting to help him. Arnold had been a general in the American army; Washington gave him the command of the fort at West Point, on the Hudson River,[23] and trusted him as though he was his brother.

Arnold deceived Washington, however, and secretly offered to give up the fort to the British. We call a person who is false to friends and country a traitor. It is the most shameful name we can fasten on such a person. Arnold was a traitor; and if the Americans could have caught him, they would have hanged him. But he was cunning enough to run away and escape to the British. Now he was burning houses and towns in Virginia, and doing all

22 Cowpens: See Map 25, p. 141.
23 Hudson River: See Map 24, p. 130.

that he could—as a traitor always will—to destroy those who had once been his best friends. He wanted to stay in Virginia and assist Cornwallis; but that general was a brave and honorable man: he despised Arnold and wanted nothing to do with him.

A young French nobleman named Lafayette[24] had come to help the Americans against the British. Cornwallis laughed at him and called him a "boy"; but he found that General Lafayette was a boy who knew how to fight! The British commander moved toward the seacoast and Lafayette followed him. At length, Cornwallis shut himself up with his army in Yorktown.[25]

### Washington marches against Yorktown and takes it ... and the army of Cornwallis

Washington and his army were near New York City, watching the British there. The French king had done as he agreed, and had sent warships and soldiers to help the Americans; but so far, they had been unable to do much. Now was the chance. Before the British knew what Washington was up to, he sent the French war-ships down to Yorktown to prevent Cornwallis from getting away by sea. Then, with his own army and some French soldiers, Washington quickly marched south to attack Yorktown by land.

When he got there he placed his cannon around the town, and began battering it to pieces. For more than a week, he kept firing night and day. One house had over a thousand balls go through it. Its walls looked like a sieve. At last, Cornwallis could not hold out any longer, and on October 19th, 1781, his army came out and gave themselves up as prisoners.

---

24 Lafayette (Lah-fay-et').
25 Yorktown: see Map 25, p. 141.

The flags of the Revolution.

The flag with the large crosses on it, on the left, is the English flag at the time of the American Revolution. The flag on the right is the one Washington raised at Cambridge, Massachusetts, on January 2, 1776. He simply took the English flag and added 13 stripes to represent the union of the 13 English colonies. The flag in the center, with its 13 stars and 13 stripes representing the 13 states, is the first American flag following the states' declaration of independence. It was adopted by the Congress on June 14, 1777, not quite a year after the states had declared themselves independent of Great Britain. Beneath this flag is Washington's coat of arms as may be seen on the tombstone of one of his ancestors, buried in 1583, in the parish church at Sulgrave, Northamptonshire, England. The coat of arms features a Latin motto that means "The outcome justifies the deed." Some scholars think the stars and stripes on the flag of the United States came from the stars and stripes (or bars) on this ancient coat of arms.

The Americans formed a line more than a mile long on one side of the road, and the French stood facing them on the other side. The French had on bright clothes and looked very handsome; the clothes of Washington's men were patched and faded, but their eyes shone with a wonderful light—the light of victory. The British marched out slowly, between the two lines. Somehow they found it more pleasant to look at the bright uniforms of the French than to look at the eyes of the Americans.

## How the news of the taking of Yorktown was carried to Philadelphia; Lord Fairfax

People at a distance noticed that the cannon had suddenly stopped firing. They looked at each other, and asked, "What does it mean?" All at once a man appeared on horseback. He was riding with all his might toward Philadelphia, where Congress was meeting. As he dashed past, he rose in his stirrups, swung his cap, and shouted with all his might: "Cornwallis is taken! Cornwallis is taken!" Then it was the people's turn to shout;

"Cornwallis is taken!"

and they made the hills ring with the sound of their vicious: "Hurrah! Hurrah! Hurrah!"

Poor Lord Fairfax, Washington's old friend. He had always stood by the king. He was now over 90. When he heard the cry, "Cornwallis is taken!" it was too much for the old man. He said to his servant, "Come, Joe. Carry me to bed, for I'm sure it's high time for me to die."

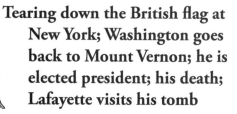

## Tearing down the British flag at New York; Washington goes back to Mount Vernon; he is elected president; his death; Lafayette visits his tomb

The Revolutionary War had lasted seven years. They had been terrible years, years of sorrow, suffering, and death. But now the end had come, and America was free. When the British left New York City, they nailed the British flag to a high pole on the wharf. A Yankee sailor soon climbed the pole, tore down the flag of England, and hoisted the stars

Hoisting the Stars and Stripes in New York.

and stripes in its place. That was more than 200 years ago. The English and Americans have become good friends, and the English people see that the Revolution ended in the way that was best for both parties.

When it was clear that there would be no more fighting, Washington went back to Mount Vernon. He hoped to spend the rest of his life there. But the country needed him, and a few years later it chose him to become the first president of the United States.

Washington was made president in New York City, the capital of the United States at the time. A French gentleman who was there tells us that Washington, standing in the presence of thousands of people, placed his hand on the Bible and solemnly swore that, with the help of God, he would protect and defend the United States of America.

Washington was elected president twice. When he died, many of the people in England and France joined Americans in mourning for him.

Lafayette came to visit the United States many years afterward. He went to Mount Vernon where Washington was buried. There he went down into the vault, and, kneeling by the side of the coffin, covered his face with his hands, and shed tears of gratitude to think that he had known such a man as Washington, and that Washington had been his friend.

Lafayette at Washinton's tomb.

## Summary

George Washington, the son of a Virginia planter, became the leader of the armies of the United States in the war of the Revolution. At the close of the war, after he had helped the American colonies gain independence from Great Britain, he was elected the first president of the new federal[26]

---

26 Federal: a system of government in which several states form a unified body for certain purposes, but maintain independence when it comes to their internal affairs.

government. His name stands today among those of the greatest men in the history of the world.

## Questions

When and where was George Washington born?

What did he learn at school?

What did he write in one of his writing books?

Why was George called "Captain George" by his classmates?

Tell the story about the colt. What did George's mother say?

Tell about George's visit to his brother and to the Fairfaxes.

Who was Lord Fairfax?

What did Lord Fairfax hire Washington to do?

What can you tell about George's surveying and his life in the woods?

What did the governor of Virginia do when Washington returned?

George journeyed to some French forts and back. What happened on that trip?

What did the Indian guide try to do?

George was knocked off a raft he and his friend built. How did that happen, and what did George do as a result?

What did the governor of Virginia order Washington to do when Washington returned?

What about Fort Necessity?

Tell about General Braddock, and about what happened to Washington.

When the war with the French and Indians ended, what did King George III determine to do?

How did the American colonists feel about that?

What did the king say?

And what did the Americans say to that?

What did the king then do?

And what happened to some tea ships as a result?

What happened in Boston and how did the king react?

What help did the people of Boston get?

What did the colonies now do?

What did the people begin to call themselves?

And what did they call the English troops?

Who commanded the British soldiers in Boston?

What did he do?

What about Paul Revere?

What did Captain Parker of Lexington say to his men as they saw the British marching toward them?

What happened at Lexington and at Concord?

Tell about the battle of Bunker Hill.

What did many Englishmen refuse to do?

Where was Colonel Washington living?

What did Congress do?

Where did Washington take command of the army?

Tell about the sharpshooters.

Tell about the march to Canada.

How did Washington take Boston?

Where did the British go?

Where did Washington go?

What did Congress do on July 4, 1776?

What happened in New York?

What about the battle of Long Island?

What did Cornwallis do?

How did Washington gain victory at Trenton?

What happened at Princeton?

What city did the British take?

Where was Washington's army at that time?

What happened at Saratoga?

What did the king of France do when he heard of the Americans' victory over the British?

What happened in the south?

Tell about Sergeant Jasper.

What is said about General Greene?

What did Cornwallis do?

Where did he go?

Who was Benedict Arnold and what did he do?

And Lafayette: who was he and what did he do?

Where did Cornwallis shut himself up with his army?

What did Washington do when he heard of where Cornwallis was?

Tell about Cornwallis' surrender.

How was the news carried to Philadelphia?

And when Lord Fairfax heard the news, how did he respond?

How long had the war lasted?

What happened in New York?

What is said of General Washington after the war?

Tell how he was made president.

What happened when he died?

Lafayette returned to Mt. Vernon many years after George Washington died. What did he do while he was there?

# Daniel Boone

### 1734-1820

### Daniel Boone; what the hunters of the west did; Boone's life in North Carolina

Boone pounding corn.

Before Washington began to fight the battles of the Revolution in the east, Daniel Boone and other famous hunters were fighting bears and Indians in what was then called the west. By that fighting, these men helped take possession of these parts of the country that the Indians had been occupying and that the King of England had told the colonists to stay out of.

Daniel Boone was born in Pennsylvania.[1] His father moved to North Carolina,[2] and Daniel helped him cut down the trees near their log cabin in the forest. Daniel ploughed the land which was thick with stumps. He hoed the corn that grew up among those stumps. And then—since there was no mill near—he pounded the corn into meal for johnny-cake.

1   He was born in Bucks County, Pennsylvania.
2   He settled near Wilkesboro, on the banks of the Yadkin River. See Map 26, p. 155.

He learned how to handle a gun almost as soon as he did a hoe. The unfortunate deer or coon that saw young Boone coming toward him would soon find out that he had seen his best days, and that he would soon have the whole Boone family sitting round him at the dinner table.

## Boone's wanderings in the western forests; his bear tree

When Daniel had grown to manhood, he wandered off with his gun on his shoulder, and crossing the mountains, entered what is now the State of Tennessee.[3] That whole country was then a wilderness, full of dangerous animals and Indians determined that white men should not take their lands. Boone engaged in many a sharp fight with both animals and men.

One of Boone's "bar" trees.

In 1760, Boone cut these words on a beech tree on the banks of Boone's Creek, near Jonesboro, Washington County, Tennessee: "D. Boon cilled a bar on tree in the year 1760." The tree eventually fell in 1920. But if it were still standing, you would see that Boone could not spell very well. He could

---

3   Tennessee: See Map 26, p. 155.

do, however, what the bear minded a good deal more,—he could shoot to kill.

**Boone goes hunting in Kentucky; what kind of game he found there; the Indians; the "Dark and Bloody Ground"**

Nine years after he cut his name on that tree, Boone, with a few companions, went to a new part of the country. The Indians called it Kentucky.[4] There he saw enough buffalo, deer, bears, and wolves to satisfy the best hunter in America.

Boone in the woods.

This region was a kind of No Man's Land, because, though many tribes of Indians used it, none claimed to own it the way Europeans would claim ownership of land. These bands of Indians were always fighting and trying to drive each other out, so Kentucky was often called the "Dark and Bloody Ground." But, much as they hated each other, they hated white men—or the "pale-faces," as they called them—still more.

---

4  Kentucky: See Map 26, p. 155.

## Indian stratagems; the owls

The white hunters were on the lookout for the Indians, but the Indians used all kinds of tricks to try to get the hunters to come near enough to shoot them before they knew the Indians were there. Once or twice, Boone heard the gobble of a wild turkey. It took a while, but then he would realize, "That's not a wild turkey; that's an Indian!" And then he took precautions so he and the Indians wouldn't get near enough to put bullets through each other's heads.

One evening an old hunter, on his way to his cabin, heard what seemed to be two young owls calling to each other. He noticed, however, that there was something not quite natural in their calls. What was stranger still, the owls seemed to be on the ground instead of being perched on trees, as all well-behaved owls would be. He crept cautiously along through the bushes till he saw something ahead that looked like a stump. He didn't altogether like the looks of the stump. He aimed his rifle at it, and fired. The stump, or what seemed to be one, fell over backward with a groan. He had killed an Indian who had been waiting to kill him.

## Boone makes the "Wilderness Road," and builds a fort at Boonesboro'

In 1775, Boone and a party of 30 men chopped a path through the forest from the mountains of Eastern Tennessee to the Kentucky River (see Map 26, p. 155), a distance of about 300 miles. This was the first path in that part of the country that led to the great west. It was called the "Wilderness Road." Over that road, which thousands of emigrants traveled afterward, Boone took his family with other settlers to the Kentucky River. There they built a fort called Boonesboro'. That fort was a great protection to all the early white

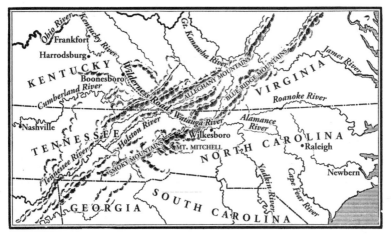

Map 26. Daniel Boone's "Wilderness Road."

settlers in Kentucky. In fact, it is hard to see how the state could have grown up without it. So in one way, we can say with truth that Daniel Boone, the hunter, fighter, and road maker, was a state builder besides.

## Boone's daughter is stolen by the Indians; how he found her

One day, Boone's young daughter was out with two other girls in a canoe on the river. Suddenly, some Indians pounced on them and carried them off.

One of the girls, as she went along, broke off twigs from the bushes, so that her friends might be able to follow her track through the woods. An Indian caught her doing it, and told her that he would kill her if she did not instantly stop. Then she slyly tore off small bits of her dress, and dropped a piece from time to time.

Boone and his men followed the Indians like bloodhounds. They picked up the bits of dress, and so easily found which way the Indians had gone. They came upon the Indians

155

just as they were sitting down to eat their supper. Creeping toward them behind the trees as softly as a cat creeps up behind a mouse, Boone and his men aimed their rifles and fired. Two of the Indians fell dead. The rest ran for their lives, and the men brought the girls safely back to the fort.

Boone trailing Indians.

## Boone is captured by Indians; they adopt him as a son

Later, Boone himself was caught and carried off by Indians. They respected his courage so much that they would not kill him, but decided to adopt him. That is, they decided to take him into the tribe as one of their own people. They would make an Indian out of him.

They pulled out all his hair except one long lock, called the "scalp-lock," which they left to grow in Indian fashion. The women and girls braided bright feathers in this lock, so that Boone looked almost pretty. Then the Indians took him down to a river. There they stripped him, and scrubbed him with all their might, to get his white blood out, as they said. Next, they painted his face in stripes with red and yellow clay, so that he looked, as they thought, handsomer than he ever had before in his life. When all had been done, they were satisfied with the appearance of their new Indian. Then they sat down to a great feast and had a good time.

### Boone escapes, but the Indians find him again; what a handful of tobacco dust did

After a time, Boone managed to escape, but the Indians did not want to let him go. One day, Boone was at work in a shed used for drying tobacco leaves. He heard a slight noise and, turning round, saw four Indians with their guns pointed at him. "Now, Boone," said they, "we got you. You will not get away this time."

"How are you?" said Boone, pleasantly; "glad to see you. Just wait a minute till I get you some of my tobacco." He gathered two large handfuls of the leaves. They were as dry as powder and crumbled to dust in his hands. Coming forward as if to give the Indians a welcome present, he suddenly sprang on them and filled their eyes, mouths, and noses with the stinging tobacco dust.

The men were half choked and nearly blinded. While they were dancing about, coughing, sneezing, and rubbing their eyes, Boone slipped out of the shed and got to a place of safety. The Indians were angry as they could be, yet they could hardly help laughing at Boone's trick; for cunning as they were, he seemed more cunning still.

### Boone's old age; he moves to Missouri; he begs for a piece of land; his grave

Boone lived to be a very old man. He had owned a good deal of land in the west, but he had lost possession of it. When Kentucky began to fill up with people and the game was killed off, Boone moved across the Mississippi into Missouri.[5] He said he went because he wanted "more elbow room" and a chance to hunt buffalo again.

---

5   Mississippi River; Missouri: See Map 27, p. 158.

But now he begged the State of Kentucky to give him a small piece of land, where, as he said, he could "lay his bones." The people of that state generously helped him to get nearly a thousand acres; but he appears to have soon lost possession of that acreage as well. If he actually did lose it, then this brave old hunter, who had opened up the way for such a multitude of emigrants to get farms at the west, died without owning a piece of ground big enough for a grave. He is buried in Frankfort, Kentucky, within sight of the river on which he built his fort at Boonesboro'.

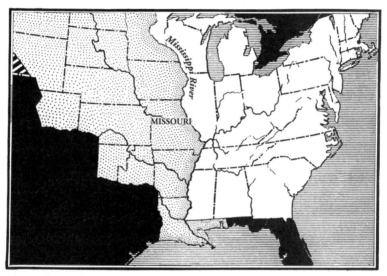

Map 27. Daniel Boone moves to what would become the state of Missouri.

## Summary

Daniel Boone, a famous hunter from North Carolina, opened up a road through the forest from the mountains of Eastern Tennessee to the Kentucky River. It was called the "Wilderness Road" and thousands of emigrants used it to go to Kentucky to settle. Boone helped lead the building project for the fort at Boonesboro', Kentucky, and went there to live.

That fort protected the settlers against the Indians, and so helped that part of the country to grow until it became the State of Kentucky.

## Questions

Tell about Daniel Boone. How did he help his father?

Where did he go when he became a man?

What did he cut on a beech tree?

Where did he go after that?

What is said of the Indians in Kentucky?

How did the Indians try to trick white settlers so they could get rid of them?

Tell about the two owls.

Tell about the Wilderness Road.

What do you know of the fort at Boonesboro'?

Tell about Boone's daughter and the other girls who were stolen by the Indians. What happened?

Tell what happened when Boone was captured by Indians and they adopted him.

Tell the story of the tobacco dust.

What did Boone do when he became old?

What did Kentucky get for him?

Where is he buried?

# Governor William Tryon
# and Governor John Sevier[1]

### 1729-1788; 1745-1815

## Governor William Tryon; the battle of Alamance[2]

William Tryon was the British governor of North Carolina from 1765 till 1771. Tryon prevailed upon the North Carolina legislature to raise taxes so he could build a home for himself. But it was not an ordinary home. Rather, it was so ornate, many people referred to it as a palace: "Tyron's Palace."

Not only did they have to pay for Tryon's expensive house, but many citizens in the west of North Carolina had to deal with corrupt local officials who enriched themselves at taxpayers' expense. These officials would falsify tax records and charge the citizens double taxes. They engaged in other corrupt practices as well.

Eventually, some of the settlers called themselves Regulators and vowed to pay no more taxes. They also began to use violence against the men they believed were using their political offices for personal gain.

When tax-collectors came to collect taxes, the Regulators drove them away. The Regulators whipped one of the governor's friends with a rawhide[3] whip. At one point, they invaded the colonial court while it was in session. They grabbed the officials in the court whom they believed were corrupt, beat these men mercilessly, and then dragged them through the

---

1 Sevier (Se-veer'): he was born in Rockingham County, Virginia.
2 Alamance River (Al'uh-mants): see Map 26, p. 155.
3 Rawhide: untanned leather ... which means it is stiff, rough, and, usually, rather heavy.

town. They smashed the court building and set things in the courtroom that are too horrible to describe. Then they attacked the judge's house and the Anglican Church building. After destroying all the furniture in the judge's house and drinking all his wine, they then burned the house to the ground.

Governor Tryon decided he had to do something about the Regulator movement. So he led a force of about 1,000 soldiers on a mission to the west. The soldiers and the Regulators met in May of 1771 near the Alamance River. Their confrontation is now known as the Battle of Alamance.

Nearly 2,000 (and some say as many as 6,000) Regulators were present when the governors' troops arrived. The Regulators were not heavily armed. As with so many civil rebellions, they were hoping their numbers alone might convince the governor to back down.

But that was not to be. A few of the Regulators were able to capture two militiamen and take them prisoner. At this, Governor Tryon told the Regulators that they were "displaying open arms and rebellion" and that, if they did not disperse, his troops would have to take action.

The Regulators refused to go their way. And so, the next morning, the governor himself shot one of the Regulators. At that, both sides joined the battle.

When the smoke had cleared, nine militiamen had died, and about the same number of Regulators were dead as well. The governor's forces also took seven of the Regulators prisoner—men whom they would hang about a month later.

## James Robertson leaves North Carolina and goes west

After the Battle of Alamance, James Robertson and his family made up their minds that they would no longer live where Governor Tryon ruled. They resolved to go across the mountains into the western wilderness. Sixteen other families joined Robertson's and went with them.

It was a long, hard journey, for they had to climb rocks and find their way through deep, tangled woods.

The men went ahead with their axes and their guns. The older children followed, driving the cows. Last of all came the women with the little children, along with beds, pots, and kettles all packed on the backs of horses.

Robertson with his party crossing the mountains on their way to Tennessee.

## The emigrants settle on the Watauga River[4] in Tennessee

When the little party had crossed the mountains into what is now the northeast corner of the State of Tennessee, they found a delightful valley. A stream of clear sparkling water flowed

4   Watauga River (Wuh-taw'guh): see Map 26, p. 155.

through this valley. It was called the Watauga River. The air of the valley was sweet with the smell of wild crabapples.

The emigrants built their new homes on the banks of the Watauga. Their houses were simple rough log huts. But they were clean and comfortable. When the settlers put up these cabins, they chopped down every tree near them that they thought might be big enough for an Indian to hide behind. They knew they might have to fight Indians; but they preferred to do that than be robbed by tax collectors. Governor Tryon could not reach them in the wilderness. As far as they were concerned, they were free—free as the deer and the squirrels were. That one thought made them contented and happy.

## John Sevier goes to settle at Watauga; what he and Robertson did

In 1773, the year after this little settlement was made, John Sevier went from Virginia to Watauga, as it was called. He and James Robertson, the leader of the group already there, soon became strong friends. They began hunting and working together.

After a while, they called a meeting of the settlers and agreed on some laws, so that everything in the village might be done decently and in order; for although these people lived in the woods, they had no notion of living like wild beasts.

The State of Tennessee grew out of this settlement on the Watauga River. About five years after he settled in Watauga, James Robertson moved once more. He and a friend traveled overland for almost two months to arrive on the banks of the Cumberland River and create the foundation for the City of

Nashville[5] beginning on December 25, 1890. Sevier became the first governor of the new state.

## Summary

The administration of British Governor William Tryon of North Carolina seemed so corrupt that many people in the western part of the colony decided to move even further west, into a portion of North Carolina that has now become the State of Tennessee.

James Robertson of North Carolina and John Sevier of Virginia emigrated across the mountains to the western wilderness. They settled on the Watauga River. That settlement, with others made later, grew into the State of Tennessee. John Sevier became the state's first governor.

## Questions

Why was colonial North Carolina's Governor Tryon so despised?

What happened on the Alamance River?

Where did James Robertson take his own and 16 other families?

Where did they settle?

Why did they like to be there?

What state grew out of the Watauga settlement?

What did John Sevier become?

---

5   Nashville, Tennessee: See Map 26, p. 155.

# General Rufus Putnam
### 1738-1824

**What General Putnam did for Washington, and what the British said of Putnam's work**

When the British gained control of Boston in the time of the Revolution, Washington asked Rufus Putnam, who was a great builder of forts, to help him drive them out. Putnam set to work one dark, stormy night, and built a fort on some high land[1] that overlooked Boston Harbor.

On the lookout.

When the British commander woke up the next morning, he saw the American cannon pointed at his ships. He was so astonished that he could scarcely believe his eyes. "Why," said he, "the rebels have done more in one night than my whole army could have done in a week." Another officer, who had

---

1  High land: known as Dorchester Heights; now South Boston.

command of the British vessels, said, "If the Americans hold that fort, I cannot keep a ship in the harbor."

Well, the Americans did hold that fort, and the British had to leave Boston. Next to General Washington, General Rufus Putnam was the man who made them go; for not many officers in the American army could build a fort like he could.

### General Putnam builds the *Mayflower*; goes down the Ohio River and makes the first settlement in Ohio

After the war was over, General Putnam left with a company of people from New England to make a settlement on the

"Down the Ohio".

Ohio River.[2] In the spring of 1788, he and his emigrants built a boat at a place just above Pittsburgh. They named this boat the *Mayflower* because, just as the Pilgrims who had come to America almost 170 years before, these people were traveling west to make a new home for themselves.

At that time there was not a white settler in what is now the State of Ohio. Most of that country was covered with thick woods. There were no roads through those woods. There was not a steamboat or railroad either. And, of course, there were no airplanes!

If you look on the map and follow down the Ohio River from Pittsburgh, you will come to a place where the Muskingum[3] joins the Ohio.[4] That's where the *Mayflower* stopped and where the emigrants landed and began to build their settlement.

## What the settlers named their town; the first Fourth of July celebration; what Washington said of the settlers

During the Revolutionary War, Queen Mary of France was the United States' firm friend, and she was very kind and helpful to Dr. Franklin when he went to France on their behalf. A number of the emigrants who joined General Putnam had fought in the Revolution, and after thinking things over, they decided to name their town Marietta,[5] in honor of the queen.

---

2   Ohio River: See Map 28, p. 171.
3   Muskingum River: See Map 28, p. 171.
4   Ohio: See Map 28, p. 171.
5   The queen's full name in French was *Marie Antoinette*. The name *Marietta* is made up from the first and the last parts of her name. Marietta: See Map 28, p. 171.

When the Marietta settlers celebrated the Fourth of July, Major Denny, who commanded a fort just across the river, came to visit them. He said, "These people appear to be the happiest folks in the world." President Washington said that he knew many of them and that he believed they were just the kind of people to succeed. He was right; for these people, with those who came later to build the city of Cincinnati,[6] were the ones who laid the foundation of the great and rich State of Ohio.

## Fights with the Indians; how the settlers held their town; Indian Rock; the "Miami Slaughter House"

The people of Marietta had hardly begun to feel at home in their little settlement before a terrible war with the Indians broke out.

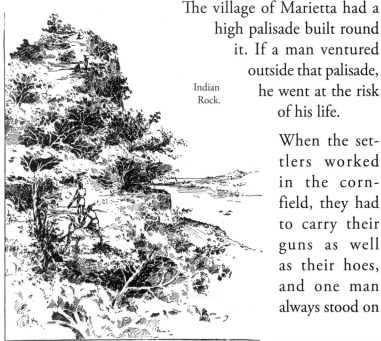

Indian Rock.

The village of Marietta had a high palisade built round it. If a man ventured outside that palisade, he went at the risk of his life.

When the settlers worked in the cornfield, they had to carry their guns as well as their hoes, and one man always stood on

6   Cincinnati, Ohio: See Map 28, p. 171.

top of a high stump in the middle of the field, to keep a sharp lookout.

There was a high rock on the Ohio River below Marietta that the settlers called Indian Rock. It got its name because the Indians used to climb up to the top and watch for emigrants coming down the river in boats. When they saw a boat, they shot guns at it hoping to leave it full of dead or wounded people. In western Ohio, on the Miami River,[7] the Indians killed so many settlers that the settlers called that part of the country the "Miami Slaughter House."

## What General Wayne did

President Washington sent a man to Ohio to make the Indians beg for peace. His name was General Wayne. He had fought in the Revolution, and fought so furiously that he was called "Mad Anthony Wayne." The Indians said he never slept. They named him "Black Snake," because the black snake is the quickest and boldest snake there is in the woods, and in a fight with any other creature of his kind he is pretty sure to win the day. General Wayne defeated the Indians and pushed them out of a very large part of Ohio. After that, white emigrants poured into Ohio by thousands.

## Summary

General Rufus Putnam and a company of emigrants settled Marietta, Ohio, in 1788. The town was named in honor of Queen Marie Antoinette of France, who had helped the American cause during the Revolution. Marietta was the first town built in what is now the State of Ohio. After General

---

7  Miami River: See Map 28, p. 171.

Wayne conquered the Indians, that part of the country rapidly increased in population.

## Questions

What did General Rufus Putnam do for Washington?

Where did General Putnam go in 1788?

What is said of Ohio at that time?

Where did the *Mayflower* stop?

What is said of Queen Mary of France?

What did the settlers name their town?

What did Washington say about the settlers?

What did these people do?

What is said about the Indians?

What about Indian Rock?

What was the country on the Miami River called?

What is said about General Wayne?

What did the Indians call him?

Why did they give him that name?

What did the Indians agree to do?

What happened after that?

# General George Rogers Clark

### 1752-1818

## The British in the west; their forts; hiring Indians to fight the settlers

Map 28. The British forts at Detroit, Kaskaskia, and Vincennes, … and the line of Clark's march.

While Washington was fighting the battles of the Revolution in the east, the British in the west were not sitting still. They had a number of forts in the Wilderness.[1] One of these forts was at Detroit, in what is now Michigan; another was at Vincennes,[2] in what is now Indiana; a third fort was at Kaskaskia,[3] in what is now Illinois.

Colonel Hamilton, the British commander at Detroit, was determined to drive the American settlers out of the west. In the beginning of the Revolution, the American colonists resolved to hire the Indians to fight for them, but the British found that they could more readily hire the Indians than the colonists could. (After all, the king had forbidden the American colonists to move west of the Allegheny Mountains—so that the Indians would remain free from the colonists' interference.) And so Britain got the Indians' help.

---

1 Wilderness: land that was unsettled or only partly settled by Europeans. See Map 29, p. 193.
2 Vincennes (Vin-senz'). See Map 28, p. 171.
3 Kaskaskia (Kas-kas'kee-uh). See Map 28, p. 171.

The Indians did their work in ways that sent fear through the hearts of many settlers. In general, the Indians did not come out and do battle openly. Instead, they crept up secretly, by night, and attacked the farmers as they slept in their homes. They would kill the male settlers, burn their cabins, and, often, carry off women and children as prisoners. The greater part of the people in England hated this sort of war. They begged the king not to hire the Indians. George III was not a bad-hearted man; but he had fully made up his mind to conquer the American rebels, even if he had to hire Indians to help him do it.

## George Rogers Clark gets help from Virginia and starts to attack Fort Kaskaskia

Daniel Boone had a friend in Virginia named George Rogers Clark, who believed that he could take the British forts in the west and drive the British out of all that part of the country. Virginia then owned most of the Wilderness. For this reason, Clark went to Patrick Henry, governor of Virginia, and asked for help. The governor liked the plan, and let Clark have money to hire men to go with him and try to take Fort Kaskaskia to begin with.

Clark started in the spring of 1778 with about 150 men. They built boats just above Pittsburgh[4] and floated down the Ohio River, a distance of over 900 miles. When they landed in what is now Illinois, they set out for Fort Kaskaskia.

## The march to Fort Kaskaskia; how a dance ended

It was a hundred miles to the fort, and half of the way the men had to find their way through thick woods that were

---

4   Pittsburgh: see Map 28, p. 171.

Clark looking on at the dance.

full of underbrush, briers, and vines. The British thought the fort was perfectly safe from attack. So they had left it in the care of a French officer. Clark and his band reached Kaskaskia at night. They found no one to stop them. The soldiers in the fort were having a dance, and the Americans could hear the merry music of a violin and the laughing voices of girls.

Clark left his men just outside the fort, and, finding a door open, he walked in. He reached the room where the fun was going on and, stopping there, he leaned against the doorpost and looked on. The room was lighted with torches; the light of one of the torches happened to fall full on Clark's face. An Indian sitting on the floor caught sight of him; he sprang to his feet and gave a terrific war-whoop. The dancers stopped as though they had been shot. The women screamed. The men ran to the door to get their guns. Clark did not move, but said quietly, "Go on; only remember you are dancing now under Virginia, and not under Great Britain." The next moment the Americans rushed in, and Clark and his "Long Knives," as the Indians called his men, had full possession of the fort.

### How Fort Vincennes was taken; how the British got it back again; what Francis Vigo[5] did

Clark wanted to march next against Fort Vincennes, but he didn't have enough men.

Father Gibault,[6] a French Catholic priest, was living at Kaskaskia at the time. Clark had been kind to him, and, as a result, Gibault felt kindly disposed toward Clark. Gibault said, "I will go to Vincennes for you, and I will tell the French, who hold the fort for the British, that the Americans are their real friends and that, in this war, the Americans are in the right."

Gibault went as he had suggested. The French soldiers listened to him. As a result, they hauled down the British flag and ran up the American flag in its place without a single shot being fired!

The next year the British, led by Colonel Hamilton of Detroit, got the fort back again. When Clark heard of it he said, "Either I must take Hamilton, or Hamilton will take me." Just then, Francis Vigo, a trader at St. Louis, came to see Clark at Kaskaskia. Hamilton had held Vigo as a prisoner, so Vigo knew all about Fort Vincennes. He said to Clark, "Hamilton has only about 80 soldiers. You can take the fort, and I will lend you all the money you need to pay your men what you owe them."

### Clark's march to Fort Vincennes; the "Drowned Lands"

Clark, with about 200 men, started for Vincennes. The distance was nearly 150 miles. The first week, everything went

---

5   Vigo (Vee'-go).
6   Gibault (Zhe-bo').

on pretty well. It was in the month of February, the weather was cold, and it rained a good deal, but the men did not mind that. They would get soaked through during the day; but at night they built roaring log fires, gathered round them, roasted their buffalo meat or venison, smoked their pipes, told hilarious stories, and sang jolly songs.

But the next week, they got to a branch of the Wabash River.[7] There they found that the constant rains had raised the streams so much that they had overflowed their banks. In fact, the whole area was under water three or four feet deep. This flooded country was called the "Drowned Lands": before Clark and his men had crossed them they were nearly drowned themselves.

## Wading on to victory

For about a week the Americans had to wade in ice-cold water, sometimes waist deep, sometimes nearly up to their chins. While wading, the men were obliged to hold their guns and powder-horns above their heads to keep them dry. Now and then a

Wading through flood.

man would stub his toe against a root or a stone and would go sprawling headfirst into the water. When he came up,

---

7  Wabash River: See Map 28, p. 171.

puffing and blowing from such a dive, he was lucky if he still had his gun. For two days no one could get anything to eat; but hungry, wet, and cold, they kept moving slowly on.

The last part of the march was the worst of all. They were now near the fort, but they still had to wade through a sheet of water four miles across.

Clark took the lead and plunged in. The rest, shivering, followed. A few looked as though their strength and courage had given out. Clark saw this, and calling to Captain Bowman—one of the bravest of his officers—he ordered him to kill the first man who refused to go forward.

At last, with numbed hands and chattering teeth, all got across. But some of them were so weak and blue with cold that they could not take another step. They fell flat on their faces in the mud. These men were so nearly dead that no fire seemed to warm them. Clark ordered two strong men to lift each of these poor fellows up, hold the dying man between them by the arms, and force him to run until he began to get warm. By doing this, Clark was able to save every one.

### Clark takes the fort; what the American rebels got by his victory; his grave

After a long and desperate fight, Clark took Fort Vincennes and hoisted the Stars and Stripes over it in triumph. The British never got it back again. Most of the Indians were now glad to make peace, and to promise to behave themselves.

By Clark's victory, the Americans got possession of the whole western wilderness up to Detroit. When the Revolutionary War came to an end, the British did not want to give up any part of the American continent beyond the territory of the 13 states on the Atlantic coast. The Americans, however said, "The whole west, clear to the Mississippi, is ours; we fought for it; we took it; we hoisted our flag over its forts, and *we mean to keep it.*" And they did keep it.

There is a grass-grown grave in a burial-ground in Louisville, Kentucky. It has a small head-stone marked with the letters G. R. C., and nothing more. That is the grave of General George Rogers Clark, the man who did more than anyone else to get for the American states the west (or what was called the west at that time).

Clark's grave.

## Summary

During the Revolutionary War, a small number of men under the command of George Rogers Clark of Virginia, captured Fort Kaskaskia in Illinois, and Fort Vincennes in Indiana. Clark drove out the British from that part of the country, and when peace was made, the American states kept the west—that is, the country as far as the Mississippi River—as part of the United States. Had it not been for Clark and his brave men, the American states might not have gotten that territory.

## Questions

The British had forts in the west. The forts were of interest and concern to the Americans who wanted independence from Britain. Where were the three forts that were of particular interest to Captain George Rogers Clark of Virginia?

The British government hired Indians to fight against their rebelling colonies. What were some of the most despised methods the Indians used in order to fight?

What did Clark undertake to do?

Tell how he went down the Ohio.

Tell how he marched on Fort Kaskaskia.

What happened when he got there?

What did Clark say to the people in the fort?

How did Clark's forces take Fort Vincennes?

What did the British do the next year?

Tell about Francis Vigo.

What did Clark and his men start to do?

How far off was Fort Vincennes?

Tell about the first part of the march.

What lands did they come to?

Tell how the men waded.

How did Clark save the lives of some of the men?

Did Clark take the fort?

What did the Americans get possession of by this victory?

What happened at the end of the Revolutionary War?

What did the Americans say?

What is said of the grave at Louisville, Kentucky?

What did Clark get for the Americans?

# Eli Whitney

1765-1825

## The name cut on a door

For over a hundred years, the door on a small wooden farm building near Westborough, Massachusetts[1] held a boy's name. It appeared just as he cut it with his pocketknife in the late 1700s.

Here is a picture of the door with the name. If the boy had

added the date of his birth, he would have cut the figures 1765. But we can imagine that, just as he got to that point, his father appeared and said rather sharply: "Eli, don't be cutting that door."

"No, sir," Eli may have answered with a start; and, shutting his knife, perhaps he hurried off to get the cows or to do his chores.

## What Eli Whitney did in his father's workshop; the fiddle

Eli Whitney's father used that little wooden building as a kind of workshop, where he mended chairs and did many other small jobs. Eli liked to go to that workshop and make little things for himself. Among other things, he made water-

---

1  Westborough, Massachusetts: See Map 24, p. 130.

wheels and windmills. As a result of all this practice, it was as natural for him to use tools as it was to whistle.

Once when Eli's father was gone from home for several days, the boy kept very busy in the little shop. When Mr. Whitney came back, he asked his housekeeper, "What has Eli been doing?"

"Oh," she replied, "he has been making a fiddle." His father shook his head, and said that he was afraid Eli would never get on much in the world. But Eli's fiddle, though it was rough-looking, was well made. It had music in it, and the neighbors liked to hear it. Somehow it seemed to say through all the tunes anyone played on it, "*Whatever is worth doing, is worth doing well.*"

## Eli Whitney begins making nails; he goes to college

When Eli was fifteen, he began making nails. Machines today can make a thousand nails a minute or more; but Eli made his, one by one, by pounding them out of a long, slender bar of red-hot iron. Whitney's hand-made nails were not handsome, but they were strong and tough, and as the Revolutionary War was then going on, he was able to sell all he could make.

When the war ended, the demand for nails was not so great. That's when Whitney laid down his hammer and said, "I am going to college." He had no money; but he worked his way through Yale College, partly by teaching and partly by doing little jobs with his tools. A carpenter who saw him at work one day noticed how neatly and skillfully he used his tools. "There was one good mechanic spoiled when you went to college," he said.

## Whitney goes to Georgia; he stops with Mrs. General Greene; the embroidery frame

When the young man had completed his course of study, he went to Georgia to teach in a gentleman's family. On the way to Savannah, he became acquainted with Mrs. Greene, the widow of the famous General Greene of Rhode Island.[2] General Greene had done such excellent fighting in the south during the Revolution that, after the war was over, the State of Georgia gave him a large piece of land near Savannah.

Mrs. Greene invited young Whitney to her house. Since he had been unable to get a teaching position with the family he had intended to serve, he was very glad to accept Mrs. Greene's invitation. While he was there, he made her an embroidery frame. It was much better than the old one she had been using, and she thought Whitney was wonderfully skillful.

## A talk about raising cotton, and about cotton seeds

Not long after this, a number of cotton planters were at Mrs. Greene's house. In speaking about raising cotton, they said that whoever could invent a machine to strip cotton seeds out of the cotton pods would make a fortune.

Why? Because what we call raw cotton or cotton wool has a great number of little green seeds clinging to it as it grows in the field. Before the cotton wool can be spun into thread and woven into cloth, those seeds must be pulled off.

At that time, planters set black slaves to do this work. When they had finished their day's labor of gathering the cotton in the cotton field, the men, women, and children would

---

2   Rhode Island: see Map 24, p. 130.

sit down and pick off the seeds, which stick so tightly that getting them off is no easy task.

After the planters had talked awhile about this work, Mrs. Greene said, "If you want a machine to do it, you should apply to my young friend, Mr. Whitney. He can make anything."

"But," said Mr. Whitney, "I have never seen a cotton plant or a cotton seed in my life"; for it was not the time of year, then, to see it growing in the fields.

### Whitney gets some cotton wool; he invents the cotton-gin; what that machine did

After the planters had gone, Eli Whitney went to Savannah and hunted about until he found, in some store or warehouse, a little cotton wool with the seeds left on it. He took

Slaves gathering cotton in the field.

this back with him and set to work to make a machine that would strip off the seeds.

Whitney's first contrivance for pulling cotton seeds out of the cotton wool.

He said to himself, "If I fasten some upright pieces of wire in a board, and have the wires set very close together, like the teeth of a comb, and then if I pull the cotton wool through the wires with my fingers, the seeds, being too large to come through, will be torn off and left behind." He tried it, and found that the cotton wool came through without any seeds on it. "Now," he said, "if I make a wheel and cover it with short steel teeth, shaped like hooks, those teeth would pull the cotton wool through the wires better than my fingers do, and very much faster.

Carrying cotton to the cotton gin.

He made such a wheel. It was turned by a crank. And it did the work perfectly. So in the year 1793, he invented the machine the planters wanted.

Before that time, it used to take one slave all day to clean a single pound of cotton of its seeds by picking them off one by one. But Eli Whitney's cotton gin,[3] as he called it, could clean a thousand pounds in a day.

## Price of common cotton cloth today; what makes it so cheap; "King Cotton"

Today nothing is much cheaper than common cotton cloth. You can buy it for two dollars a yard. But before Whitney invented his cotton-gin it sold for a dollar and a half a yard—the equivalent of over $32 a yard in today's money. Before Whitney's cotton gin came along, planters in the south raised very little cotton, since few people could afford to buy it. But after the cotton gin was made, the planters kept making their fields bigger and bigger. At last they raised so much more of this plant than of anything else, that they said, "Cotton is king." It was Eli Whitney who built the throne for that king; and although he did not make a fortune by his machine, he did receive a good deal of money for the use of it in some of the southern states.

The "Star-Spangled Banner."

In the war of 1812, British warships attacked Fort McHenry, one of the defenses of Baltimore. Francis Scott Key, a native of Maryland, was at that time being detained on board a British man-of-war. He anxiously watched the battle during the night. Before dawn, the firing ceased. Key had no means of telling whether the British had taken the fort until the sun rose. Then, to his joy, he saw the American flag still floating triumphantly above the fort. That meant that the British had failed in their attack.

Key, in his delight, hastily wrote the song we know as the Star Spangled Banner. He wrote it on the back of a letter he had in his pocket. The song was printed almost at once, and in a few weeks, it was known and sung from one end of the United States to the other.

Later, Mr. Whitney built a gun factory near New Haven, Connecticut, at a place called Whitneyville, now part of Hamden. Whitney made at that factory thousands of the

---

3  Gin: a shortened form of the word *engine*, meaning a machine, something that does work.

muskets that the American troops used in the United States' second war with England in 1812.

## Summary

Eli Whitney of Westborough, Massachusetts, invented the cotton gin in 1793. The gin is designed to make it easy to pull off the green seeds from cotton wool, so that it can be easily woven into cloth. The cotton gin made thousands of cotton planters and cotton manufacturers rich and, by it, cotton cloth became so cheap that everybody could afford to use it.

## Questions

What did Eli Whitney cut on the door of his father's workshop?

What did Eli make in that workshop?

What did he make while his father was away?

What did his father say?

What did Eli's fiddle seem to say?

What did Eli make next?

How did he make his nails?

Where did he go after he gave up making nails?

When he left college, where did he go?

What did he make for a lady?

What did the cotton-planters say?

What must be done to raw cotton before it can be made into cloth?

Who did this work?

What did Mrs. Greene say to the planters?

What did Mr. Whitney say?

What did he do?

Tell how he made his machine. What did he call it?

How many pounds of cotton would his cotton gin clean in a day?

How much could one slave clean?

What happened to the price of cotton cloth as a result of Mr. Whitney's invention?

What did the planters say about cotton?

Who built the throne for King Cotton?

What did Mr. Whitney build at Whitneyville?

What did he make there?

# Thomas Jefferson
1743-1826

**How much cotton New Orleans sent to Europe; Eli Whitney's work; who it was that bought New Orleans and Louisiana for the United States**

In the mid to late 1800s, the city of New Orleans,[1] near the mouth of the Mississippi River,[2] sent more cotton to England and Europe than any other city in America.

If you had visited that city and gone down to the riverside, you would have seen thousands of

Thomas Jefferson.

---

1 New Orleans: See Map 30, p. 194.
2 Mississippi River: See Map 30, p. 194.

cotton bales[3] piled up, and hundreds of black laborers loading them on ocean steamers.

Before Eli Whitney invented his machine, American growers sent hardly a bale of cotton abroad. Afterward, they sent so much in one year that the bales could be counted in the millions. If they were laid end to end, in a straight line, they would reach clear across the American continent from San Francisco to New York, and then across the ocean from New York to Liverpool, England.

It was Eli Whitney, more than any other man, who helped to build up this great trade. But at the time when he invented his cotton gin, the United States did not own New Orleans, or, for that matter, any part of Louisiana[4] or of the country west

Jefferson's home
at Monticello.

---

3   A bale or bundle of cotton was somewhat more than five feet long, and generally weighed from 400 to 550 pounds. The cotton crop of the United States in 1891 amounted to more than 8,650,000 bales. Laid end to end, in a straight line, these bales would extend more than 8000 miles.

4   Louisiana: See Map 30, p. 194.

of the Mississippi River. The man who bought New Orleans and Louisiana for the United States was Thomas Jefferson.

## Who Thomas Jefferson was; Monticello;[5] how Jefferson's slaves met him when he came home from Europe

Thomas Jefferson was the son of a rich planter who lived near Charlottesville in Virginia.[6] When his father died, he came into possession of a plantation of nearly 2,000 acres of land and 40 or 50 black slaves on it.

Slaves meeting Jefferson.

5   Monticello (Mon-tih-chel'lo).
3   Charlottesville, Virginia: See Map 25, page 141.

There was a high hill on the plantation. Jefferson called it Monticello, or little mountain. There he built a fine house. From it, he could see the mountains and valleys of the Blue Ridge for an immense distance. No man in America had a more beautiful home, or enjoyed it more, than Thomas Jefferson. Jefferson treated his slaves about as well as any slaveholder. He was generally kind to them. Once, when he came back from France where he had been staying for a long time, the slaves went to meet his carriage. They walked several miles down the road. When they caught sight of the carriage, they shouted and sang with delight.

When Jefferson reached Monticello and got out, the slaves took him in their arms, and, laughing and crying for joy, they carried him into the house. Perhaps no king ever got such a welcome as that; for that welcome was not bought with money: it came from the heart. Yet Jefferson said he looked forward to the time when every slave in the country might be set free.

### Thomas Jefferson hears Patrick Henry speak at Richmond

Jefferson was educated to be a lawyer. He was not a good public speaker, but he liked to hear men who were.

Just before the begin-ning of the Revolu-

"We must fight!"

tionary War, in 1775, the people of Virginia sent men to the city of Richmond[7] to hold a meeting in old St. John's Church. They met to decide what they should do about defending those rights that the king of England had refused to grant to his American subjects.

One of the speakers at that meeting was a famous Virginian named Patrick Henry. When Henry got up to speak, he looked pale, but his eyes shone like coals of fire. He made a great speech.

He said, "We must fight! I repeat it, sir,—we must *fight!*" The other Virginians agreed with Henry; and George Washington and Thomas Jefferson—along with other noted men who were present at the meeting—began at once to make ready for battle.

## Thomas Jefferson writes the Declaration of Independence; how it was sent through the country

Shortly after this meeting, the great war began. In a little over a year from the time when the first battle was fought, Congress asked Thomas Jefferson, Benjamin Franklin, and some others to write the Declaration of Independence. Jefferson wrote almost every word of it. He was called the "Pen of the Revolution," for he could write quite as well as Patrick Henry could speak.

The Declaration was printed and carried by men mounted on fast horses all over the United States. When people heard it, they rang church bells and sent up cheer after cheer. General Washington had the Declaration read to all the soldiers in his army, and if powder had not been so scarce, we can be quite sure they would have fired off every gun for joy.

---

7   Richmond, Virginia: See Map 25, p. 141.

## Jefferson is chosen president of the United States; what he said about New Orleans

A number of years after the war was over, Jefferson was chosen president of the United States. While he was president, he did something for the country that will never be forgotten.

At the time, the city of New Orleans and the lower part of the Mississippi River belonged to the French. At that time, the United States only reached west as far as the Mississippi River. But since New Orleans stands near the mouth of the river, the French could stop any vessels that wanted to go out to sea. They could stop any vessels that wanted to come in as well. As far as that part of America was concerned, then, the American settlers were like a man who owns a house while another man owns the doors to it. The man who has the door could say to the owner of the house, "You must pay me so many dollars every time you go out and every time you come in this way."

Jefferson understood that as long as the French held the door of New Orleans, the western United States would not be free to send goods down the river and across the ocean to Europe. He said the United States needed that door, no matter how much it cost.

## Jefferson buys New Orleans and Louisiana for the United States

In keeping with his Constitutional right to negotiate treaties, President Jefferson sent James Monroe (a former student of his and a future president) and Robert R. Livingston (one of the men who signed the Declaration of Independence) to Paris. He wanted them to negotiate a purchase agreement

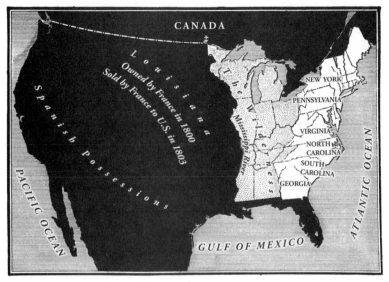

Map 29. The extent of the United States at the close of the Revolution and when Jefferson became president (1801).

by which the United States would buy from France the city of New Orleans and the nearby coastal lands.

Napoleon Bonaparte[8] ruled France at the time. He needed money to buy warships and other supplies so that he could fight England. "I will not sell New Orleans only," he said. "If you want New Orleans, then you must purchase all of Louisiana besides, for $15 million."

If you look at Map 30, you will see that, at that time, Louisiana (highlighted by polka dots) was not simply a good-sized state. It was an immense country. It reached clear back to the Rocky Mountains. It included more land than what all of the United States, together, owned east of the Mississippi River.

Napoleon's offer was unbelievably generous. Monroe and Livingston had been authorized to spend up to $10 million for New Orleans and the land around it. So $15 million for

---

8   Napoleon Bonaparte (Nuh-po'lee-un Bo'nuh-part).

Map 30. How much larger the territory of the United States became as a result of the Louisiana Purchase in 1803. (The Oregon country is marked in bars to show that its ownership was disputed; both England and the United States claimed ownership rights.)

a land area that proved 16 times larger: that sounded very good, indeed.

And so in 1803 President Jefferson and his representatives signed an agreement with France to purchase it.[9] Through the Louisiana Purchase, the United States added so much land that they now had more than twice as much as they had before. They had acquired the whole Mississippi River, the city of New Orleans, and more than three-quarters of a million square miles of territory—land that, today, includes great cities like Denver, Oklahoma City, Kansas City, Omaha, Tulsa, Wichita, St. Louis, and more.

## Death of Jefferson; the words cut on his gravestone

Jefferson lived to be an old man. He died at Monticello on the Fourth of July, 1826, just 50 years, to the day, after he had signed the Declaration of Independence. John Adams,

---

9    Of course, Congress had to *approve* the agreement. And it did so.

who had been president immediately before Jefferson, died just a few hours later. So America lost two of her great men on the same day.

Jefferson was buried at Monticello. He asked to have these words, with some others, cut on his gravestone:

Here Lies Buried

THOMAS JEFFERSON,

Author of the
Declaration
of
American Independence.

## Summary

Thomas Jefferson of Virginia wrote the Declaration of Independence. After he became president of the United States, he initiated and authorized the purchase of Louisiana for the United States. The Louisiana Purchase gave Americans the right to send ships to sea by way of the Mississippi River, which now belonged to the United States. Louisiana added so much land that it more than doubled the size of the United States.

## Questions

Before Whitney invented his cotton gin how much cotton did the United States send abroad?

Which president arranged for the United States to purchase New Orleans and Louisiana from France?

Who was Thomas Jefferson?

What is said about Monticello?

Tell how Jefferson's slaves welcomed him home.

For what profession was Jefferson educated?

Tell about Patrick Henry. What did he say?

What did Washington and Jefferson do?

What did Jefferson write?

As a result, what name did he receive?

How was the Declaration of Independence sent to all parts of the country?

What was Jefferson chosen to be?

At the time he was elected, how far did the territory of the United States extend toward the west?

What could the French say to Americans who tried to ship goods via the Mississippi River?

The book suggests the western territories of the United States were like what, while France was like what?

What did Jefferson say?

How much did the United States pay for the Louisiana Territory?

How large was Louisiana at that time?

How much land did the United States get out of the bargain?

What else did they get?

When did Jefferson die?

What other great man died on the same day?

What words did Jefferson have cut on his gravestone at Monticello?

# Robert Fulton

1765-1815

**What some people said about Louisiana; a small family in a big house; settlements in the west; the country beyond the Mississippi River**

Even before the United States bought the great Louisiana country, they had more land than they knew what to do with. After they had purchased it, it seemed to some people as though the United States would not know what to do with all of that land for more than a hundred years. Such people thought that the United States were like a family that lives in a house much too large for their needs but, who, not contented with that, buys their neighbor's house, which is bigger still, and adds it to the one they already own.

If travelers in those days went across the Allegheny Mountains[1] to the west, they found some small settlements in Ohio, Kentucky, and Tennessee, but hardly any outside of those. What are now the great states of Indiana, Illinois, Michigan, and Wisconsin were, at that time, a wilderness. And this was also true of what are now the states of Alabama[2] and Mississippi.[3]

If the same travelers had pushed across the Mississippi River on foot or on horse-back—for there were no railroads, cars, or airplanes at that time—they would hardly have found a white person outside of what was then the little town of

---

1  Allegheny Mountains: See Map 25, page 141.
2  Alabama: See Map 30, page 194.
3  Mississippi: See Map 30, page 194.

St. Louis.[4] The country stretched away west for more than a thousand miles, with nothing in it but wild animals and Indians. In much of it there were no trees, no houses, no human beings. If you shouted as hard as you could in that solitary land, the only reply you would hear would be the echo of your own voice. It was like shouting in an empty room—it made it seem lonelier than ever.

## Emigration to the west, and the man who helped that emigration

But despite the expectations, during the next hundred years after the United States made its Louisiana Purchase, that great empty land of the far west filled with people. Thousands upon thousands of emigrants moved there. They built towns and cities, railroads and telegraph lines. And what made that migration possible?

One man helped to do a great deal to make that movement possible. His name was Robert Fulton. He saw how difficult it was for people to get west; for if emigrants wanted to go with their families in wagons, they had to chop roads through the forest. That was slow, hard work. Fulton found a way that was quick, easy, and cheap. Let's see who he was, and how he found that way.

## Robert Fulton's boyhood; the old scow; what Robert did for his mother

Robert Fulton was the son of a poor Irish farmer in Pennsylvania.[5] He did not care much for books, but he liked to draw pictures with pencils that he hammered out of pieces of lead.

---

4   St. Louis, Missouri: See Map 30, page 194.
5   Fulton was born in Little Britain (now called Fulton) in Lancaster County, Pennsylvania. See Map 24, page 130.

Like most boys, he was fond of fishing. He used to go out in an old scow, or flat-bottomed boat, on a river near his home. He and another boy would push the scow along with poles.

But Robert said, "There is an easier way to make this boat go. I can put a pair of paddle-wheels on her, and then we can sit com-fortably on the seat and turn the wheels by a crank. He tried it, and found that he was right. The boys now had a boat that suited them very nicely.

Robert Fulton's paddlewheel scow.

When Robert was 17, he went to Philadelphia. His father was dead, and he earned his living and helped his mother and sisters by painting pictures. He stayed in Philadelphia until he was 21. By that time, he had saved up money enough to buy a small farm for his mother so that she could have a home of her own.

## Fulton goes to England and to France; his iron bridges; his diving boat, and what he did with it in France

Soon after buying the farm for his mother, young Fulton went to England and then to France. He stayed in those countries for 20 years. In England, Fulton built some famous iron bridges, but he was more interested in boats than in anything else.

While he was in France, he made what he called a diving boat. It would travel under water nearly as well as it would on top, so that wherever a fish could go, Fulton could follow him. His interest in building such a boat was to make war in a new way. When a swordfish[6] attacks a whale, he slips under him and stabs the whale with his sword. Fulton said, "If an enemy's warship should come into the harbor to do mischief, I can get into my diving boat, slip under the ship, fasten a torpedo[7] to it, and blow the ship sky high."

Napoleon Bonaparte liked nothing so much as war, and he let Fulton have an old vessel to see if he could blow it up. Fulton tried it, and everything happened as he expected: nothing was left of the vessel but the pieces.

However, when Napoleon examined the submarine, he noticed that it leaked a bit. As a result, he decided the submarine could not possibly work, and so he declared Fulton a swindler.

## What Fulton did in England with his diving-boat; what he said about America

Since the French weren't interested, Fulton went to England to try his luck there. He went out in his diving boat and fastened a torpedo under a vessel. When the torpedo exploded, the vessel, as he said, went up like a "bag of feathers," flying in all directions.

The English government paid Fulton a great deal of money for showing them what he could do in this way. Then they offered to give him even more—in fact, to make him a very rich man—as long as he would promise never to let any other country know just how he blew vessels up. But Fulton said, "I am an American; and if America should ever want to use my diving boat in war, she shall have it first of all."

---

6  Swordfish: the name given to a large fish which has a sword-like weapon, several feet in length, projecting from its upper jaw.

7  Torpedo: here, a can filled with gunpowder, and constructed so that it could be fastened to the bottom of a vessel.

## Fulton makes his first steamboat

But while Fulton was doing these things with his diving boat, he was always thinking of the paddlewheel scow he had used when a boy. *I turned those paddlewheels by crank,* he thought, *but what is to hinder my putting a steam engine into such a boat, and making it turn the crank for me?* If he could create such a mechanism, he would have created a steamboat. Such boats had already been tried, but, for one reason or another, they had not become very popular. Robert R. Livingston was still in France, and he helped Fulton build his first steamboat. It was put on a river there; it moved, and that was about all.

## Robert Fulton and Mr. Livingston go to New York and build a steamboat; the trip up the Hudson River

But Robert Fulton and Mr. Livingston both believed that a steamboat could be built that would go, and that would keep going. So they went to New York and built one there.

In the summer of 1807, a great crowd gathered to see Fulton's steamboat start on her voyage up the Hudson River. They joked and laughed as crowds will at anything new. They called Fulton a fool and Livingston another. But when Fulton, standing on the deck of his steamboat, waved

Fulton's steamer leaves New York for Albany.

his hand, and the wheels began to turn, and the vessel began to move up the river, that was when the crowd became silent with astonishment. Now it was Fulton's turn to laugh, and in such a case the man who laughs last has a right to laugh the loudest.

Up the river Fulton kept going. He passed the Palisades; he passed the Highlands;[8] still he kept on, and at last he reached Albany, 150 miles above New York.

Nobody before had ever seen such a sight as that boat moving up the river without the help of oars or sails; but from that time, people saw it every day. When Fulton got back to New York in his steamboat, everybody wanted to shake hands with him—the crowd, instead of shouting fool, now whispered among themselves, *He's a great man—a very great man, indeed.*

## The first steamboat in the west; the Great Shake

Four years later Fulton built a steamboat for the west. In the autumn of 1811 it started from Pittsburgh and with down the Ohio River, then down the Mississippi to New Orleans. The people of the west had never seen a steamboat before, and when the Indians saw the smoke puffing out, they called it the "Big Fire Canoe."

On the way down the river there was a terrible earthquake. In some places, it changed the course of the Ohio so that where there had been dry land there was now deep water, and where there had been deep water there was now dry land. One evening, the captain of the "Big Fire Canoe" fastened his vessel to a large tree on the end of an island. In the morning the people on the steamboat looked out, but could not tell

8   Highlands: See Map 11, p. 43.

where they were; the island had gone: the earthquake had carried it away. The Indians called the earthquake the "Big Shake": it was a good name, for it kept on shaking that part of the country, and it did all sorts of damage for weeks.

## The "Big Fire Canoe" on the Mississippi; the fight between steam and the Great River; what steamboats did; Robert Fulton's grave

When the steamboat reached the Mississippi, the settlers on that river said that the boat would never be able to go back, because the current is so strong. At one place, a crowd had gathered to see her as she turned against the current in order

The "Big Fire Canoe" on the Mississippi.

to come up to the landing place. An old black man stood watching the boat. It looked as if in spite of all the captain could do, she would be carried downstream, but at last, the engines conquered, and the boat came up to the shore. Then the old black man could hold his joy no longer. He threw up his ragged straw hat and shouted, "Hoo-ray! Hoo-ray! The old Mississippi's just got her master this time, sure!"

Soon steamboats began to run regularly on the Mississippi, and in the course of a few years they began to move up and down the Great Lakes[9] and the Missouri River.[10] Emigrants could now go to the west and the far west quickly and easily. They had Robert Fulton to thank for that.

Robert Fulton lies buried in New York, in the shadow of the tower of Trinity Church. There is no monument or marker over his grave, but he has a monument in every boat on every great river and lake in America.

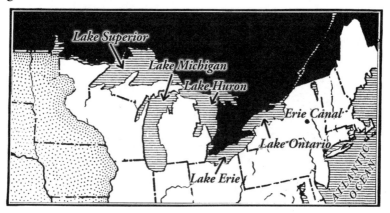

Map 31. The Great Lakes.

## Summary

In 1807, Robert Fulton of Pennsylvania built the first steamboat that ran on the Hudson River. Four years later, he built the first one to navigate the rivers of the west. His boats helped to fill the whole western country with settlers.

---

9  Great Lakes: Michigan, Superior, Huron, Erie, Ontario: See Map 31, p. 204.
10  Missouri River: See Map 30, p. 194.

# Questions

What did some people say about the United States' purchase of Louisiana?

What did they think the United States were like?

If people traveled west at that time, what would they find?

What is said of the country west of the Mississippi?

Who helped emigration to the west?

What did he discover?

Tell about Robert Fulton as a boy.

Tell about his paddle-wheel scow.

What did Robert do for his mother?

Where did he go?

How long did he stay abroad?

Tell about his diving boat.

What did he do with it in France?

What about in England?

What did the English people offer him?

What did Fulton say?

Where did Fulton make and try his first steamboat?

Tell about the steamboat he made in New York.

How far up the Hudson did it go?

Tell about the first steamboat at the west.

What did the Indians call it?

What happened on the way down the Ohio River?

Tell about the steamboat on the Mississippi River.

What is said of steamboats in the west?

What about emigrants?

Where is Fulton buried?

Where is his monument?

# General William Henry Harrison

### 1773-1841

Map 32. Location of the Tippecanoe battle grounds.

**A great battle between settlers and Indians; how the Indians felt about being forced to leave their homes; the story of the log**

The year 1811, in which the first steamboat went west, a great battle was fought between European settlers and Indians. The battleground was on the Tippecanoe[1] River in what is now the State of Indiana.

The Indians fought because they wanted to stop the European settlers from taking the land away from them. They felt just like an old chief did: he had been forced to move over and over again by the white men. One day, a military officer came to the chief's wigwam to tell him that he and his tribe must move still further west.

The chief said, "General, let's sit down on this log and talk it over." So they both sat down.

After they had talked a short time, the chief said, "Please move a little further that way; I haven't room enough." The officer moved along.

In a few minutes the chief asked him to move again, and he did so.

---

1  Tippecanoe (Tip'-eh-kuh-noo'): see Map 32, p. 206.

Presently the chief gave him a push and said, "Do move further along, won't you?"

"I can't," said the general.

"Why not?" asked the chief.

"Because I've got to the end of the log," replied the officer.

"Well," said the Indian, "now you see how it is with us. You white men have kept pushing us until you have pushed us clear to the end of our country, and yet you come now and say, 'Move on, move on.'"

"Move on."

## What Tecumseh[2] and his brother, the Prophet,[3] tried to do

A famous Indian warrior named Tecumseh determined to band the different Indian tribes together and drive out the white men from the west.

Tecumseh had a brother called the Prophet, who believed he could tell what would happen in the future. He said, "The white traders come here, give the Indians whiskey, get them

---

2  Tecumseh (Teh-kum'suh).
3  Prophet (prof'et): one who tells what will happen in the future.

drunk, and then cheat them out of their lands. Once we owned this whole country. Now, if an Indian strips a little bark off of a tree to shelter him when it rains, a white man steps up with a gun in his hand and says, 'That's my tree; let it alone, or I'll shoot you.'"

Then the Prophet said to the Indians, "Stop drinking 'fire-water,'[4] and you will have strength to kill off the 'pale-faces' and get your land back. When you have killed them off, I will bless the earth. I will make pumpkins grow to be as big as wigwams, and the corn shall be so large that one ear will be enough for a dinner for a dozen hungry Indians."

The Indians liked to hear these things. They wanted to taste those pumpkins and that corn, and so they got ready to fight.

## Who William Henry Harrison was; the march to Tippecanoe; the Prophet's sacred beans; the battle of Tippecanoe

At this time, William Henry Harrison[5] was governor of the Indiana territory. He had fought under General Wayne[6] in his war with the Indians in Ohio.

Everybody knew Governor Harrison's courage, and the Indians all respected him; but he tried in vain to prevent the Indians from going to war. The Prophet urged them on at the north, and Tecumseh had gone south to persuade the Indians there to join the northern tribes.

Governor Harrison saw that a battle would soon be fought, so he started with his soldiers to meet the Indians. He marched

---

4  Fire-water: the Indian name for whiskey.
5  William Henry Harrison was born in Berkeley, Charles City County, Virginia, about 25 miles below Richmond. His father, Governor Harrison of Virginia, was one of the signers of the Declaration of Independence.
6  See "What General Wayne did" on p. 169.

The Battle of Tippecanoe.

to the Tippecanoe River, and there he stopped.

While Harrison's men were asleep in the woods, the Prophet told the Indians not to wait, but to attack the soldiers at once. In his hand he held up a string of beans. "These beans," he told the Indians, "are sacred.[7] Come and touch them, and you will be safe. No white man's bullet will hit you." The Indians hurried up in crowds to touch the wonderful beans.

Now, said the Prophet, "Let each one take his hatchet in one hand and his gun in the other, and creep through the tall grass till he gets to the edge of the woods. The soldiers lie there fast asleep. When you get close to them, spring up and at them like a wildcat at a rabbit."

The Indians started to do this, but a soldier on guard saw the tall grass moving as though a great snake was gliding

---

7   Sacred: something holy, or set apart for religious uses.

through it. He fired his gun at the moving grass. With a yell, up sprang the whole band of Indians, and rushed forward. And in a moment, the battle began.

Harrison won the victory. He not only killed many of the Indians, but he marched against their village, set fire to it, and burned it to ashes.

After that, the Indians in that part of the country would not listen to the Prophet. They said, "He is a liar; his beans didn't save us."

The battle of Tippecanoe was a turning point in relations between Indians and white settlers. It prevented the Indian tribes from uniting and beginning a great war all through the west. Governor Harrison received high praise from the white settlers for what he had done, and he was made a general in the United States army.

## Tecumseh takes the Prophet by the hair; the War of 1812; General Harrison's battle in Canada; President Harrison

When Tecumseh came back from the south, he was terribly angry with his brother for fighting before he was ready to have him begin. He seized the Prophet by his long hair, and shook him like a terrier[8] shakes a rat. Tecumseh then left the United States and went to Canada to help the British, who were getting ready to fight the Americans a second time.

The next year (1812) the United States began its second war with England. It is called the War of 1812. One of the chief reasons why the Americans fought was because the British would not let the American merchant ships alone.

---

8   Terrier (tär´ee-er): a kind of small hunting dog.

The British navy would stop American ships at sea, take American sailors off of them, and then force these men to serve in British warships against the French.

In the course of the War of 1812, the British burned the Capitol at Washington. But a grander building rose from its ashes. General Harrison fought a battle in Canada in which he defeated the British and killed Tecumseh, who was fighting on the side of the English.

Many years after this battle, the people of the western United States said, "We must have the 'Hero of Tippecanoe' serve as president of the United States." They went to vote for him with songs and shouts, and he was elected. A month after he had gone to Washington, President Harrison died (1841), and the whole country was filled with sorrow.

## Summary

In 1811 General Harrison gained a great victory over the Indians at Tippecanoe in Indiana. By that victory, many people believe he saved the west from a terrible, long, drawn-out battle between white immigrants and Indians. In the War of 1812, General Harrison beat the British in a battle in Canada and killed Tecumseh. Many years later, General Harrison was elected president of the United States.

## Questions

Where was a great battle fought between European settlers and Indians in 1811?

How did the Indians feel about the west?

Tell the story of the log.

What did Tecumseh determine to do?

Tell about the Prophet.

Who was William Henry Harrison?

Tell about the battle of Tippecanoe.

Tell about the sacred beans.

What did the Indians say about the Prophet after the battle?

What was the result of the battle of Tippecanoe?

What did Tecumseh do when he got back?

Where did he then go?

What happened in 1812?

Why did the United States fight Britain?

What did General Harrison do in Canada?

What did the people of the west say?

How long did General Harrison live after he became president?

# General Andrew Jackson

1767-1845

**Andrew Jackson and the War of 1812; his birthplace; his school; wrestling-matches; firing off the gun**

The greatest battle of the United States' second war with England—the War of 1812—was led, on the American side, by General Andrew Jackson.

He was the son of a poor emigrant who came from the North of Ireland and settled in North Carolina.[1] When Thomas Jefferson wrote the Declaration of Independence in 1776, Andrew was nine years old, and his father had long been dead. He was a tall, slender, freckled-faced, barefooted boy, with eyes full of fun. The neighbors called him "Mischievous little Andy."

He went to school in a log hut in the pine woods; but he learned more things from what he saw in the woods than from the books he studied in school.

He was not a very strong boy, and in wrestling, some of his companions could throw him three times out of four. But though they could get him down without much trouble, it was quite another thing to keep him down. No sooner was he laid flat on his back, than he bounded up like a steel spring, and stood ready to try again.

He had a violent temper, and when, as the boys said, "Andy got mad all over," not many cared to face him. Once, some of his playmates secretly loaded an old gun almost up to

---

1 He settled in Union County, North Carolina, very near the South Carolina line. See Map 25, p. 141. Mecklenburg Court House is in the next county west of Union County.

the muzzle, and then dared him to fire it. They wanted to see what he would say when it kicked him over. Andrew fired the gun. It knocked him sprawling. He jumped up with eyes blazing with anger and, shaking his fist, he cried out, "If one of you boys laughs, I'll kill him." He looked as though he meant exactly what he said, and the boys thought that perhaps it would be just as well to wait and laugh some other day.

## Tarleton's[2] attack on the Americans; how Andrew helped his mother

When Andrew was 13, he learned what war means. The American states were then fighting the battles of the Revolution. A British officer named Tarleton came suddenly upon some American soldiers near the place where young Jackson lived. Tarleton had so many men that the Americans realized it was useless to try to fight, so they made no attempt to do so. The British could have taken them all prisoners but, instead, they attacked the Americans furiously with their swords. More than a hundred American men were left dead, and a still larger number were so horribly wounded that they could not be moved any distance. Such an attack was not war, for war means a fair, stand-up fight. No. It was murder. And when the people in England heard what Tarleton had done, many cried "Shame!"

There was a little log meetinghouse near Andrew's home, and it was turned into a hospital for the wounded men. Mrs. Jackson and other kindhearted women did all they could for the poor fellows who lay there groaning and helpless. Andrew carried food and water to them. He had forgotten most of the lessons he learned at school, but this was one event he would never forget.

---

2  Tarleton (Tarl'tun).

## Andrew's hatred of the Red Coats;[3] Tarleton's soldiers meet their match

From that time, when young Jackson went to the black-smith's shop to get a hoe or a spade mended, he was sure to come back with a crude spear or some other weapon he had hammered out to fight the Red Coats with.

Tarleton said that no people in America hated the British as much as those who lived where Andrew Jackson did. The reason was that no other British officer had been as cruel as "Butcher Tarleton," the name by which the Americans called him. Once, however, Tarleton's men met their match.

They were robbing a farm of its pigs and chickens, corn and hay. When they got through carrying things off, they were going to burn down the farmhouse; but one of the Red Coats, in his haste, ran against a big hive of bees and turned it over. The bees were furious. They swarmed down on the soldiers, got into their ears and eyes, and stung them so terribly that at last the robbers were glad to drop everything and run. If Andrew could have seen that battle, he would have laughed till he cried.

## Dangerous state of the country; the roving bands

Andrew knew that he and his mother lived in constant danger. Part of the people in his state were in favor of the king, and part were for liberty. Bands of armed men, belonging sometimes to one side, and sometimes to the other, went roving about the country. When they met a farmer, they would stop him and ask, "Which side are you for?" If he did not answer to suit them, the leader of the party would cry

---

3   Red Coats: this nickname was given by the Americans to the British soldiers because they wore bright red coats.

out, "Hang him up!" In an instant, one of the band would cut down a long piece of wild grapevine, twist it into a noose, and throw it over the man's head. The next moment he would be dangling from the limb of a tree. Sometimes the band would let him down again. Sometimes they would ride on and leave him hanging there.

## Playing at battle; what Tarleton heard about himself

Even the children saw and heard so much of the war that they began playing war, and fought battles with red and white corn—red for the British and white for the Americans.

At the battle of Cowpens,[4] Colonel William Washington[5] fought on the American side, and Tarleton got badly whipped and had to run. Not long afterward, he happened to see some boys squatting on the ground, with a lot of corn instead of marbles. They were playing the battle of Cowpens. A red kernel stood for Tarleton, and a white one for Colonel Washington. The boys shoved the corn this way and that; sometimes the red would win, sometimes the white. At last the white kernel gained the victory, and the boys shouted, "Hurrah for Washington—Tarleton runs!"

Tarleton had been quietly looking on without their knowing it. When he saw how the game ended, he turned angrily away. He had seen enough of "the little rebels,"[6] as he called them.

---

4 Cowpens: see Map 25, p. 141.
5 Colonel William Washington was a relative of General George Washington.
6 Rebels: the name the British gave to the Americans because they were seeking to overthrow the authority of the English king.

## Andrew is taken prisoner by the British; "Here, boy, clean those boots"; the two scars

Not long after the Americans' victory at Cowpens, Andrew Jackson was taken prisoner by the British. The officer in command of the soldiers had just taken off his muddy boots. Pointing to them, he said to Andrew, "Here, boy, clean those boots."

Andrew replied, "Sir, I am a prisoner of war, and it is not my place to clean boots."

The officer, in a great passion, whipped out his sword and struck a blow at the boy. It cut a gash on his head and another on his hand. Andrew Jackson lived to be an old man, but the marks of that blow never disappeared. He carried the scars to his grave.

## The prisoners in the yard of Camden jail; seeing a battle through a knot-hole

Andrew was sent with other prisoners to Camden, South Carolina,[7] and shut up in the jail yard. There, many fell sick and died of smallpox.[8]

Jackson and the Officer's boots.

---

7   Camden, South Carolina: See Map 25, p. 141.
8   Smallpox: a highly contagious and deadly disease. Some experts believe it may have killed more people than any other disease in all of world history.

One day, some of the prisoners heard that General Greene—the greatest American general in the Revolution, next to Washington—was coming to fight the British at Camden. Andrew's heart leaped with joy, for he knew that if General Greene won he would set all the prisoners at liberty.

General Greene, with his little army, was on a hill in sight of the jail, but there was a high, tight board fence round the jail yard, and the prisoners could not see them. With the help of an old razor, Andrew managed to dig out a knot from one of the boards. Through that knothole he watched the battle.

The American troops were beaten in the fight, and Andrew saw their horses, with empty saddles, running wildly about. Then the boy turned away, sick at heart. Soon after, he was seized with the smallpox. He would have died of it if his mother had not succeeded in getting him set free.

### Mrs. Jackson goes to visit the American prisoners at Charleston; Andrew loses his best friend; what he said of her

In 1781, Mrs. Jackson made a journey on horseback to Charleston, 160 miles away. She went to carry some comforts to the American prisoners. They were starving and dying of disease in the crowded and filthy British prison ships in the harbor. While visiting these men, she caught a fever that was raging among them. Two weeks later, she was in her grave, and Andrew, then a lad of fourteen, stood alone in the world.

Years afterward, when he had risen to be a noted man, people would sometimes praise him because he was never afraid to say and do what he believed to be right; then Jackson would answer, "*That* I learned from my good old mother."

## Andrew begins to learn a trade; he studies law and goes west; Judge Jackson; General Jackson

Andrew set to work to learn the saddler's trade, but gave it up to study law. After he became a lawyer, he went across the mountains to Nashville, Tennessee. There he was made a judge. There were plenty of rough men in that part of the country who meant to have their own way in all things; but they soon found that they must respect and obey Judge Jackson. They could frighten other judges, but it was no use trying to frighten him.

Seeing what sort of stuff Jackson was made of, they thought they would like to have such a man lead them in battle. And so Judge Andrew Jackson became General Andrew Jackson. When the settlers got into trouble with the Indians, Jackson was happy to lead them.

## Tecumseh and the Indians of Alabama; Tecumseh threatens to stamp his foot on the ground; the earthquake; war begins

We have already seen how the Indian chief Tecumseh went south to encourage the Indians to fight the white settlers. In Alabama, he told the Indians that if they fought, they would gain a great victory.

"I see," said Tecumseh, "that you don't believe what I say, and that you don't mean to fight. Well, I am now going north to Detroit. When I get there I shall stamp my foot on the ground, and shake down every wigwam you have."

It so happened that, shortly after Tecumseh had gone north, a sharp shock of earth-quake was felt in Alabama, and the wigwams were actually shaken down by it. When the terrified Indians felt their houses falling to pieces, they ran out of them, shouting, "Tecumseh has got to Detroit!"

These Indians now believed all that Tecumseh had said. They began to attack the white people, and they killed a great number of them.

### Jackson conquers the Indians; the "Holy Ground"; Weathersford and Jackson; feeding the starving

General Jackson marched against the Indians and beat them in battle. The Indians that escaped fled to a place they called the "Holy Ground." They believed that if a white man dared to set his foot on that ground, he would be struck dead as if by a flash of lightning.

General Jackson and his men marched on to the "Holy Ground," and the Indians found that unless they made peace, they would be the ones who would be struck dead ... by Jackson's bullets.

Not long after this, a noted leader of the Indians named Weathersford rode boldly up to Jackson's tent. "Kill him! Kill him!" cried Jackson's men. But the general asked Weathersford into his tent.

"You can kill me if you want to," Weath-

General Jackson and Indian Chief Weathersford.

Battle of New Orleans.

By Act of Congress of 1794 the number of stars and stripes on the national flag was fixed at fifteen, to correspond with the whole number of states then in the Union; the flag remained unchanged until 1818, when the present arrangement was adopted, namely, thirteen stripes, and a star for every state.

ersford said to Jackson, "but I came to tell you that the Indian women and children are starving in the woods, and to ask you to help them, for they never did you any harm."

General Jackson sent Weathersford away in safety, and ordered that corn should be given to feed the starving women and children. That act showed that he was as merciful as he was brave.

## The British send warships to take New Orleans; the great battle and the great victory

These things happened during the War of 1812. About a year after Jackson's victory over the Indians, the British sent an army in ships to take New Orleans.

General Jackson now went to New Orleans to prevent the enemy from getting possession of the city.

New Orleans stands on the Mississippi River.[9] About four miles below the city, there was a broad, deep ditch that ran from the river into a swamp. Jackson saw that the British would have to cross that ditch when they marched against the city. For that reason he built a high bank on the upper side of the ditch and placed cannon along the top of the bank.

Early on Sunday morning, January 8th, 1815, the British sent a rocket whizzing up into the sky; a few minutes afterward they sent up a second one. It was the signal that they were about attack.

Just before the fight began, General Jackson walked along among his men, who were getting ready to defend the ditch. "Stand to your guns," he said. "See that every shot tells. Give it to them, boys!"

---

9   New Orleans: See Map 30, p. 194.

The "boys" did give it to them. The British soldiers were brave men. They had been in many terrible battles and they were not afraid to die. They fought desperately. They tried again and again to cross that ditch and climb the bank, but they could not do it. The fire of the American guns cut them down just as a lawnmower cuts grass.

In less than half an hour, the great battle was over. Jackson had won the victory and saved New Orleans. The Americans lost only eight killed; the British, over 2,000 killed or wounded.

The United States has never had a battle since with England.

## The United States buy Florida; General Jackson made president of the United States; the first railroad

After the battle of New Orleans, General Jackson was sent to Florida to take care of "the Indian problem."

Map 33. The light parts of this map show the extent of the United States in 1819, after they had bought Florida. The black and white bars in the northwest show that the ownership of the Oregon country was still in dispute between the United States and Great Britain.

Seminole Indians, who lived along the Florida-Georgia border would make raids in Georgia and then retreat to Florida. In late 1817, the situation came to a head when the Seminoles massacred 46 of 51 people aboard a ship. Their attack was, itself, a response to having had one of their villages in Georgia burned to the ground.

The president of the United States, James Monroe, sent General Jackson to "take care of the problem." Jackson went to Florida with a couple of thousand troops and not only subdued the Indians, but took control of Pensacola,[10] the Spanish capital of Florida. The Spanish minister protested that the American troops had no business being in Florida, but the American secretary of state replied, "Either keep the Indians in line, or we will do it for you."

Spain was more concerned about the revolutions that were taking place among its possessions in South America at the time, so, in 1819, it willingly sold Florida to the United States for $5 million. And so the United States became much larger in the south. This was the United States' second great land purchase.

Ten years after the United States got Florida, General Jackson became president of the United States. He had fought his way up. Here are the four steps: first the boy, "Andy Jackson"; then "Judge Jackson"; then "General Jackson"; last of all, "President Jackson."

Shortly after Andrew Jackson became president, the first steam railroad in the United States was built.[11] From that time, such roads kept creeping further and further west. The

---

10 Pensacola, Florida: See Map 33, p. 223

11 The first steam railroad built in the United States extended from Baltimore to Ellicott's Mills, Maryland, a distance of twelve miles. It was opened in 1830. It forms a part of the Baltimore and Ohio Railroad.

Indians had frightened the white settlers with their terrible war-whoop. Now it was their turn to be frightened, for the locomotive whistle could beat their wildest yell. They saw that white settlers were coming as fast as steam could carry them, and that they were determined to get possession of the whole land. The greater part of the Indians moved across the Mississippi. But the white settlers kept following them—and following the buffalo—further and further across the country, toward the Pacific Ocean. And the railroad followed the white settlers' tracks.

The Georgetown Loop.

Near Georgetown, Colorado.

## Summary

Andrew Jackson of North Carolina subdued the Indians in Alabama and also in Florida. In 1815, in the United

States' second war with England, General Jackson whipped the British at New Orleans, and so prevented their getting possession of that city. A few years later, partially as a result of his invasion of Florida, the United States bought Florida from Spain.

After General Jackson became president of the United States, the first steam railroad was built in the United States. Railroads helped to settle the west and build up states beyond the Mississippi.

## Questions

Who fought the greatest battle of the War of 1812?

Tell about Andrew Jackson's boyhood. Tell the story of the gun.

Tell about Tarleton.

What did Mrs. Jackson do?

What did Andrew do?

What did Andrew do at the blacksmith shop?

Tell about Tarleton's men and the bees.

What did bands of armed men use to do in the country where Andrew lived?

Tell about playing at battle.

What did Tarleton say?

Tell about Andrew and the boots.

How did Andrew see a battle through a knothole?

Tell how Andrew's mother died.

What did he say about her?

Tell about Andrew Jackson as a judge.

Why was Jackson made a general?

Tell about Tecumseh and the Alabama Indians.

After General Jackson had beaten the Indians, where did they go?

What is said about the "Holy Ground"?

What about Jackson and Weathersford?

Tell about the battle of New Orleans.

Who gained the victory?

When did the United States buy Florida?

What were the four steps in Andrew Jackson's life?

What is said about railroads?

# Professor Morse

## 1791-1872

**How they sent the news of the completion of the Erie Canal to New York City; Franklin and Morse**

The Erie Canal, in the State of New York, connected the Hudson River at Albany with Lake Erie at Buffalo. It was the greatest work of the kind in America. When the water was let into the canal from the lake, the news was flashed from Buffalo to New York City by a row of cannon, about five miles apart, which were fired as rapidly as possible one after the other. The first cannon was fired at Buffalo at ten o'clock in the morning. The last was fired at New York at half-past eleven. In an hour and a half, the sound had traveled over 500 miles. Everybody said that was wonderfully quick work. But today we could send the news in less than a second. The first man who found out how to communicate over such a distance so quickly was Samuel F. B. Morse.

How they flashed the news of the completion of the Erie Canal in 1825.

Samuel Morse was born in Charlestown, Massachusetts, about a mile from Benjamin Franklin's birthplace, the year after that great man died. Morse began his work where Franklin left off. He said to himself, "Dr. Franklin found out what lightning is. I will find out how to harness it and make it carry news and deliver messages."

Map 34. The Erie Canal.

## Morse becomes a painter; what he thought might be done about sending messages

When Samuel Morse was a little boy, he was fond of drawing pictures, particularly faces. If he could not get a pencil, he would use a pin to scratch his pictures on the furniture at school. The only pay he got for making such pictures was some sharp raps from the teacher.

After Morse became a man, he learned to paint. At one time he lived in France with several other American artists. One day they were talking of how long it took to get letters from America, and they wished the time could be shortened. Somebody spoke of how cannon had been used at the time the Erie Canal opened. Morse was familiar with all that; he had been educated at Yale College, and he knew that the sound of a gun will travel a mile while you are counting five. But quick as that is, he wanted to find something better and quicker still. He said, "Why not try lightning or electricity?

That will beat sound, for that will go more than a thousand miles while you are counting *one*."

## What a telegraph[1] is; a wire telegraph; Professor Morse invents the electric telegraph

Some time after that conversation, Mr. Morse set sail for America. On the way across the Atlantic, he was constantly talking about electricity and how a telegraph—that is, a machine that can write at a distance—might be invented. He thought about this so much that he could not sleep at night. At last, he believed that he understood how he could make such a machine.

Suppose you take a straight and stiff piece of wire as long as your desk and fasten it in the middle so that the ends will swing easily. Next, tie a pencil tight to each end. Then put a sheet of paper under the point of each pencil. Now, if you

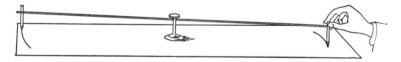

One kind of telegraph.

make a mark with the pencil nearest to you, you will find that the pencil at the other end of the wire will make the same kind of mark. Such a wire would be a kind of telegraph, because it would make marks or signs at a distance.

Mr. Morse said, "I will have a wire a mile long with a pencil, or something sharp-pointed like a pencil, fastened to the further end. The wire itself shall not move at all, but the

1 Telegraph (tel'eh-graf): this name is made up of two Greek words, the first (*tele*) means *far off*, and the second (*graph*) means *to write*. So it creates *writing at a distance*.

pencil shall, for I will make electricity run along the wire and move it."

Mr. Morse was then a professor at the University of the City of New York. He put up a wire in one of the rooms of his building, sent the electricity through it, and found that it made the pencil make just the marks he wanted it to. That meant that he had invented the *electric telegraph*. For if he could do this over a mile of wire, then what was to hinder his doing it over a hundred or even a thousand miles?

## How Professor Morse lived while he was making his telegraph

Professor Morse at work making his telegraph.

But all this was not done in a day, for this invention cost years of patient labor. At first, Mr. Morse lived in a little room by himself. That is where he worked and ate (when he could get anything to eat) and slept (if he wasn't too tired to sleep). Later, he had a room in the university.

While he was at the university, he painted pictures to get money enough to buy food; there, too, in 1839, he took the first photograph ever made in America. Yet with all his hard work, there were times when he had to go hungry, and once he told a young man that if he did not get some money he would be dead in a week—dead of starvation.

## Professor Morse gets help with his telegraph; what Alfred Vail did

But better times were coming. A young man named Alfred Vail[2] happened to see Professor Morse's telegraph. He believed it would be successful. He persuaded his father, Judge Vail, to lend him $2,000, and he became Professor Morse's partner in the work.

Mr. Vail was an excellent mechanic, and he made many improvements in the telegraph. He then made a model of it at his own expense, took it to Washington, and got a patent[3] for it in Professor Morse's name. The invention was now safe in one way, for no one else had the right to make a telegraph like his. Yet, though he had this help, Professor Morse did not make much money, for a few years later he said, "I have not a cent in the world."

## Professor Morse asks Congress to help him build a telegraph line; what Congress thought

Professor Morse now asked Congress to let him have $30,000 to construct a telegraph line from Washington to Baltimore. He felt sure that business owners would be glad to send messages by telegraph, and to pay him for his work. But many members of Congress laughed at it, and said they might as

---

2 Alfred Vail: the son of Stephen Vail, commonly known as Judge Vail, owner of the Speedwell ironworks, near Morristown, New Jersey. Judge Vail built the engines of the *Savannah*, the first steamship to cross the Atlantic.

3 Patent: a government-guaranteed right to make, use, or sell something. A patent forbids anyone other than the patent holder to enjoy these rights. As a result, the patent owners get whatever money comes from their patents. It used to be the case that inventors had to send working models of their inventions to the Patent Office in Washington.

well give Professor Morse the money to build "a railroad to the moon."

Week after week went by, and the last day that Congress would sit was reached, but still no money had been granted. Then came the last night of the last day (March 3, 1843). Professor Morse stayed in the Senate Chamber[4] of Congress until after ten o'clock; then, tired and disappointed, he went back to his hotel. He thought he would have to give up trying to build his telegraph line.

## Miss Annie Ellsworth brings good news

The next morning, Miss Annie G. Ellsworth met Morse as he was coming down to breakfast. She was the daughter of his friend who had charge of the Patent Office in Washington. She came forward with a smile, grasped his hand, and said that she had good news for him. "Congress has decided to give you money!" she said. "Surely you must be mistaken," said the professor, "for I waited last night until nearly midnight, and came away because nothing had been done."

"But," said the young lady, "my father stayed until it was quite midnight, and a few minutes before the clock struck twelve, Congress voted the money;[5] it was the very last thing that was done."

Professor Morse was then a gray-haired man over fifty. He had worked hard for years and got nothing for his labor. This was his first great success. He never said whether he laughed or cried—perhaps he felt a little like doing both.

---

4   Senate Chamber: Congress is divided into two classes—Representatives and Senators; they meet in different rooms, or chambers, in the Capitol at Washington.

5   Voted money: here the word means voted to *give* or *grant* money.

## The first telegraph line built; the first message sent; the telegraph and the telephone[6] now

When, at length, Professor Morse did speak, he said to Miss Ellsworth, "Now, Annie, when my line is built from Washington to Baltimore, you shall send the first message over it."

In the spring of 1844, the line was completed, and Miss Ellsworth sent these words over it: "*What hath God wrought!*"[7]

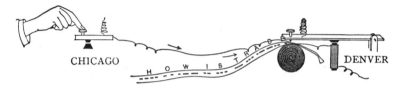

CHICAGO                    DENVER

How messages were sent by telegraph.

When the button at Chicago was pressed, the electricity passed through the wire to Denver and pressed the pen point there down onto the strip of paper as it moved over the roller. And so it made dots and dashes on the paper—dots and dashes that stood for letters. In this way, words and messages were spelled out. The message on the strip of paper above is the question, "How is trade?"

For nearly a year after that, the telegraph was free to all who wished to use it. Then a small charge was made. A very short message cost only one cent. On the first of April, 1845, a man came into the office and bought a cent's worth of telegraphing. That was all the income the company made that day for the use of 40 miles of wire.

By the late 1800s, however, there were close to 200,000 miles of telegraph lines in the United States: more than enough to reach eight times round the earth. And the messages sent

---

6    Telephone (tel'uh-fone): this name is made up of two Greek words, the first (*tele*) which means *far off*, and the second, *voice* or *sound*. So the the *telephone* means *voice* or *sound at a distance*. The telephone was invented by Professor Alexander Graham Bell of Boston; he completed it in 1876. And, of course, nowadays we have *television* ... which means *sight* or *vision at a distance*.

7    Phrase taken from Numbers 23:23 in the Bible.

brought in over $70,000 every day. And people could telegraph not only across America, but across the Atlantic Ocean by a line laid under the sea.

Professor Morse's invention made it possible for people to write by electricity; but, of course, by the late 1800s, people were able to talk by electricity from New York to Chicago or beyond. And by the 1960s, television signals were relayed around the world. Professor Morse did not live long enough to see these wonderful inventions. But they are, in some ways, improvements on his telegraph.

## Summary

Professor Morse invented the one-wire Electric Telegraph. He received much help from Mr. Alfred Vail. In 1844, Professor Morse and Mr. Vail built the first single-line telegraph in the United States, or in the world. (Separate from Morse, and unknown to Morse, two Englishmen, William Cooke and Charles Wheatstone, formed a partnership and patented a multiple-line electric telegraph in England in May 1837. They built a 13-mile multiple-wire system shortly afterward.) Morse's system extended from Washington to Baltimore. The telegraph made it possible for people to send written messages thousands of miles in a moment. By the telephone, which was invented after Professor Morse's death, people can now talk with others who are hundreds or even thousands of miles away ... and hear what they say in reply.

## Questions

Tell how they sent the news of the completion of the Erie Canal.

What did Samuel Morse say to himself?

Tell about Morse as a painter.

What did Morse want to find?

What was he talking about on his voyage back to America?

What is a telegraph?

How can you make a small wire telegraph?

What did Professor Morse make?

How did he live?

What did Morse do in 1839?

How did he get help about his telegraph?

What did he ask Congress to do?

What did some men in Congress say?

What news did Miss Annie Ellsworth bring him?

What was the first message sent by telegraph in 1844?

# General Sam Houston

1793-1863

---

## Sam Houston[1] and the Indians; Houston goes to live with the Indians

When General Jackson defeated the Indians in Alabama, a young man named Sam Houston fought under Jackson and was terribly wounded. It was thought that the brave fellow would certainly die, but his strong will carried him through, and he lived to make himself a great name in the southwest.

Although Houston fought the Indians, he was very fond of them when he was a boy, and he spent much of his time with them in the woods of Tennessee.

Long after he became an adult, his love for the Indian way of life in the forest came back to him. While Houston was governor of Tennessee, in 1829, he suddenly made up his mind to leave his home and his friends, go across the Mississippi River, and take up his abode with an Indian tribe in that part of the country. The chief, who had known him as a boy, gave him a hearty welcome. "Rest with us," he said; "my wigwam is yours." Houston stayed with the tribe for three years.

---

1  Sam Houston (Hew'ston): he always wrote his name Sam Houston; he was born near Lexington in Rockbridge County, Virginia.

**Houston goes to Texas; what he said he would do; the murders at Alamo; the flag with one star; what Houston did; Texas added to the United States; the United States' war with Mexico**

"Remember the Alamo!"

At the end of that time, Houston said to a friend, "I am going to Texas,[2] and in that new country I will make a man of myself." Texas then belonged to Mexico; and President Andrew Jackson had tried in vain to buy Texas as Jefferson bought Louisiana.

Houston said, "I will make it part of the United States." About 20,000 Americans had already moved into Texas, and

---

2   Texas: See Map 35, p. 240.

The "Lone Star" flag.

they felt as he did: they would take the land from Mexico and make it part of the United States.

The Texas settlers declared independence from Mexico, and the Mexican government fought back. General Sam Houston led the Texan soldiers in their fight for independence. In his little army, he had many noted American pioneers[3] and hunters: one of them was Colonel Travis of Alabama; another was Colonel Bowie of Louisiana, the inventor of the "bowie knife"; still another was Colonel David Crockett of Tennessee, whose motto is a good one for every young American—"Be sure you're right, then—*go ahead.*"

These men all eventually died at the hands of the Mexican army at Fort Alamo—an old Spanish church in San Antonio.[4]

Not long after that, General Houston fought a great battle near the city that is now called by his name.[5] The Mexicans had more than two men to every one of Houston's, but the Americans and Texans went into battle shouting the terrible cry *"Remember the Alamo!"* and the Mexicans fled before them. Texas then became an independent state, and elected General Houston its president. The people of Texas raised a flag having on it a single star. For this reason it was sometimes called, as it still is, the "Lone Star State."

---

3 Pioneers: those who go before to prepare the way for others; the first settlers in a country are its pioneers.
4 San Antonio: See Map 35, p. 240.
5 Houston: See Map 35, p. 240.

Texas was not contented to stand alone. She begged to join the family of the United States. This was done in 1845. But, as we shall presently see, the American settlers in Texas, with the aid of the United States army, were soon able to start a war with Mexico that, in the end, gave the United States a great deal more land at the west.

## General Sam Houston in the great war between the North and the South; what he said

We have seen the part that General Sam Houston took in getting new country to add to the United States. He lived in Texas for many years after that. When, in 1861, the great war broke out between the North and the South, General Houston was governor of Texas. He withdrew from office and went home to his log cabin in Huntsville, Texas. He refused to take any part in the war, for he loved the Union—that is, the United States as a whole, North and South together—and he said to his wife, "My heart is broken."

Map 35. The extent of the United States after they added Texas in 1845. The black and white bars show that the ownership of the Oregon country was still in dispute between the United States and Great Britain.

Before the war ended, he was laid in his grave.[6]

## Summary

General Sam Houston of Tennessee led the people of Texas in their war for independence from Mexico. The Texans gained the victory, and made their country an independent state with General Houston as its president. After a time, Texas was added to the United States. The United States then had a war with Mexico, and added a great deal more land in the west. General Houston died during the war between the North and the South.

## Questions

Tell about Sam Houston and the Indians.

Where did Houston go after he became governor of Tennessee?

Where did Houston go next?

What did he say he would do about Texas?

What was David Crockett's motto?

What is said about Fort Alamo?

What happened in the battle between the American settlers in Texas and the Mexican army?

What did Texas become?

To what office was Houston elected?

What is said about the Texas flag?

When was Texas added to the United States?

What war then broke out?

What did the United States gain by that war?

What is said about General Houston and the great war between the North and the South—the American Civil War?

---

6   General Houston was buried at Huntsville, about 80 miles northwest of the city of Houston, Texas.

# Captain Robert Gray

1755-1806

**Captain Gray goes to the Pacific coast to buy furs; he is the first to carry the Stars and Stripes round the globe**

Not long after the war of the Revolution had come to an end, some merchants of Boston sent out two vessels to Vancouver Island[1] on the northwest coast of the United States. They sent the vessels to buy furs from the Indians who lived in Vancouver.

The names of the vessels were the *Columbia* and the *Lady Washington*. They sailed round Cape Horn into the Pacific.

Mount Hood, Oregon.

---

1    Vancouver (Van-Koo'ver): part of it is seen off the west coast of Canada at the very north edge of Map 36, p. 243.

Captain Robert Gray was commander of one of these vessels. He had no difficulty in getting all the skins he wanted since the Indians seemed glad to sell them for very little. In one case, a chief let the captain have 200 sea-otter skins—which were worth about $8,000 in Massachusetts—in exchange for an old iron chisel.

Map 36. The extent of the United States after they added the Oregon Country in 1846.

After getting this valuable cargo of furs, Captain Gray then sailed in the *Columbia* for China, where he bought a quantity of tea. He then went to the south and west—round the Cape of Good Hope—and eventually returned to Boston in the summer of 1790. He had been gone about three years, and he was the first man who had carried the American flag clear round the globe.

## Captain Gray's second voyage to the Pacific coast; he enters a great river and names it the Columbia; the United States claims the Oregon country; the United States acquires Oregon in 1846

Emigrants on their way to Oregon in the 1840s.

Captain Gray did not stay long at Boston, for he sailed again that autumn in the *Columbia* for the Pacific coast, to buy more furs.

This time, he stayed on the coast for a long time. In the spring of 1792, he entered and sailed up a great river a distance of nearly 30 miles. He seems to have been the first white man who had ever actually entered it. He named the vast stream the Columbia River,[2] from the name of his vessel. It is the largest American river south of Alaska that empties into the Pacific Ocean.[3]

Captain Gray returned to Boston and gave an account of his voyage of exploration; this led Congress to claim the

---

2   Columbia River: See Map 36, p. 243.
3   The Yukon River in Alaska is larger than the Columbia.

country through which the Columbia flows[4] as part of the United States.

After Captain Gray had been dead for 40 years, the United States did, in fact, come into clear possession of the immense territory then called the Oregon Country.[5] It was through what Captain Gray had done that the United States got its first claim to that country which now forms the states of Oregon and Washington.

## Summary

Captain Robert Gray was the first person to carry the American flag round the world. He achieved that feat in 1790. Then, in 1792, he entered and named the Columbia River. Because he did that, the United States claimed the country—called the Oregon Country—through which the Colombia River runs. In 1846, the United States added the Oregon Country to its possessions. That territory now forms the two states of Oregon and Washington.

## Questions

Tell about Captain Gray's voyage to the Pacific coast.

What did he buy there?

He was first to carry something round the globe. What was it?

Tell about his second voyage.

What did he do in 1792?

What happened after Captain Gray returned to Boston?

What happened in 1846?

What two states were made out of the Oregon Country?

---

4    According to the rules concerning the "right of discovery" that were still operating at that time among the Western "Christian" nations (see Footnote 11, p. 10), when someone explored a river, that usually gave the government of his nation the right to claim the territory that provided water to the river.

5    Oregon Country: See Map 36, p. 243.

# Captain Sutter

1803-1880

## Captain Sutter and his fort; how the captain lived

In 1844, at the time when Professor Morse sent his first message by telegraph from Washington to Baltimore, Captain J. A. Sutter, an emigrant from Switzerland, was living near the Sacramento River in California. California belonged to Mexico at the time. The governor of that part of the country had given Captain Sutter an immense piece of land; and the captain had built a fort at a point where a stream that he named the American River joins the Sacramento River. People then called the place Sutter's Fort, but today it is the City of Sacramento, the capital of the State of California.

Map 37. Coloma, Sutter's Fort and surrounding territory.

In his fort, Captain Sutter lived like a king. He owned land enough to make a thousand fair-sized farms. He had 12,000 head of cattle, more than 10,000 sheep, and over 2,000 horses and mules. Hundreds of laborers worked for him in his wheat-fields, and 50 well-armed soldiers guarded his fort. Quite a number of Americans had built houses near the fort. They thought that the time was coming when all that country would become part of the United States.

## Captain Sutter builds a saw-mill at Coloma;[1] a man finds some sparkling dust

About forty miles up the American River was a place that the Mexicans called Coloma, or *beautiful*. There was a good fall of water there and plenty of big trees to saw into boards, so Captain Sutter sent a man named Marshall to build a saw-mill there. The captain needed such a mill very badly, for he wanted lumber with which to build and to fence his fields.

Marshall set to work, and before the end of January, 1848, he had built a dam across the river and got the sawmill half done. One day, as he was walking along the bank of a ditch they had dug back of the mill to carry off excess water, he saw some bright yellow specks shining in the dirt. He gathered a little of the sparkling dust, washed it clean, and carried it to the house. That evening, after the men had come in from their work on the mill, Marshall said to them, "Boys, I believe I've found a gold mine." They laughed, and one of them said, "I reckon not; no such luck."

## Marshall takes the shining dust to Captain Sutter; what he did with it, and how he felt about the discovery

A few days after that, Marshall went down to the fort to see Captain Sutter. "Are you alone?" he asked when he saw the captain.

"Yes," he answered.

"Well, won't you oblige me by locking the door? I have something I want to show you." The captain locked the door, and Marshall took a little parcel out of his pocket, opened it, and poured some glittering dust on a paper he had spread out.

---

1   Coloma (Kuh-lo'muh): see Map 37, p. 246.

"See here," said he. "I believe this is gold, but the people at the mill laugh at me and call me crazy."

There are three very interesting things about gold. In the first place, it is very heavy, heavier even than lead. Next, it is very tough.

Is it gold?

If you hammer a piece of iron long enough, it will break to pieces, but you can hammer a piece of gold until it is thinner than the thinnest tissue paper, so that if you hold it up you can actually see light shining through it. Last of all, if you pour strong acids on gold, acids that will eat into other metals and change their color, those acids will have no more effect on gold than an acid like vinegar has on a piece of glass.

For these and other reasons, most people think that gold is a very beautiful metal, and the more they see of it, especially if it is their own, the better they are pleased with it.

Well, Captain Sutter examined the yellow dust carefully. He weighed it. He pounded it flat. He poured some strong acid on it. The shining dust stood all these tests. It was very heavy, it was very tough, and the sharp acid did not hurt it. Captain Sutter and Marshall both felt sure that it was *gold*.

But, strange to say, the captain was not pleased. He wanted to build an American settlement and have it called by his name. He did not care for a gold mine—why should he?

He had everything he wanted without it. He was afraid, too, that if gold should be discovered in any quantity, thousands of people would rush in; they would dig up his land and quite likely take it all away from him. We will see shortly whether he was right or not.

## War with Mexico; Mexico lets the United States have California and New Mexico; "gold! gold! gold!"; what happened at Coloma; how California was settled; what happened to Captain Sutter and to Marshall

While these things were happening in California, the United States had been at war with Mexico for two years (1846-1848). Texas and Mexico could not agree about the south-

Map 38. The United States' territories in 1848, after Mexico transferred its Alta California and Nuevo Mexico states to them.

western boundary line[2] of the new state. Texas wanted to push that line as far south and west as possible so as to have more land, and Mexico, of course, wanted to push it as far north and east as possible so as to give as little land as necessary.

"Gold! From the American River!"

This dispute soon led to war between the United States and Mexico. Soon after gold was discovered at Coloma—and before the news spread—the war between the United States and Mexico ended. The United States forced Mexico to turn over not only all the land the people of Texas had asked for, but much more as well. They got Mexico's states of Alta California and Nuevo Mexico—land from which a number of states in the Union have since been made.[3] Though the transfer was made under threat of military conquest, the United States did agree to pay Mexico $15 million for the land. They also agreed to relieve Mexico from having to pay $3.25 million to American citizens who claimed Mexico owed them such money.

---

2  Southwestern boundary line: the people of Texas held that their state extended south and west as far as the Rio Grande River. Mexico insisted that the boundary line was at the Nueces River, which is further north and east.

3  Namely: California, Nevada, Utah, part of Wyoming, and large parts of Colorado, New Mexico, and Arizona. See Map 38, p. 249.

In May, 1848, a man came to San Francisco holding up a bottle full of gold-dust in one hand and swinging his hat with the other. As he walked through the streets, he shouted with all his might, "Gold! gold! gold! from the American River."

That is when the rush for Coloma began. Every man had a spade and a pick-axe. In a little while, the beautiful valley was dug so full of holes that it looked like an empty honeycomb.

The next year, 100,000 people poured into California from all parts of the United States; so the discovery of gold filled up that part of the country with emigrants years before they would have gone if no gold had been found there.

Captain Sutter lost all his property. He would have died poor if the people of California had not given him money to live on.

Marshall was still more to be pitied. He got nothing by his discovery. Years after he had found the shining dust, someone wrote to him and asked him for his photograph. He refused to send it. He said, "My likeness ... is, in fact, all I have that I can call my own. And I feel like any other poor wretch:[4] I want *something* for self."

## How the United States bought more land; its growth since the Revolution

Long before Captain Sutter died, the United States bought from Mexico another great piece of land, marked on the map by the date of its purchase: 1853. This territory is generally known as the Gadsden Purchase.[5] A number of years later,

---

4  Wretch: here a very unhappy and miserable person.
5  See Map 39, p. 249. It was called the Gadsden Purchase because General James Gadsden of South Carolina bought it from Mexico for the United States. It included what is now part of Southern Arizona and N. Mexico.

Map 39. The United States' territories in 1853 after they had added the land called the Gadsden Purchase, bought from Mexico. The Gadsden Purchase is marked on the map by the date it was made: 1853.

in 1867, the United States bought the territory of Alaska from Russia.

If you look at Map 29 on page 193 and compare it with the maps that follow, you will see how the United States territories grew over the next 100 years. At the time of the Revolution, there were just 13 states in the Union. Their territory stretched along the Atlantic, and, with the country west of them, extended as far as the Mississippi River.

With this territory as a base, the Union bought the great territory of Louisiana (see Map 30, p. 194), which was subsequently divided into many states. Then the United States bought Florida (1819; see Map 33, p. 223), annexed Texas (1845; see Map 35, p. 240); negotiated the acquisition of the Oregon territory that is now the great states of Oregon and Washington (1846; see Map 36, p. 243); and forced Mexico to sell the territory that now comprises the southwestern part of the Union (1848; see Map 38, p. 249).

Scene on an Alaskan river.

The Union then bought the land known as the Gadsden Purchase (1853; see Map 39 on p. 252) and Alaska (1867; see Map 40 on p. 254). Subsequently, it annexed the Hawaiian Islands (1898; these have since become the 50th state in the Union), and has acquired—and sometimes given up—a number of other territories. Among those it claims right now are Puerto Rico (1898), Guam (1898), the U.S. Virgin Islands (1917), and the Northern Mariana Islands (1978).

## The United States' eight steps

If you count up the territorial additions through Hawaii, Guam and Puerto Rico, you will see that, beginning with Louisiana in 1803, and ending with the last three island acquisitions in 1898, they make just eight steps.

Map 40. The territorial growth of the United States from the time of the Revolution to 1867.

There is a story of a giant who was so tall that at one long step he could go more than 20 miles. The United States, however, in seven steps, traveled over 3,000 miles to Alaska, and, in eight steps, well over 5,000 miles to its last state, Hawaii. If you include the Union's farthest territories, however, you are looking at a span of over 9,000 miles between Puerto Rico and Guam. The United States has one foot in Puerto Rico, in the North Atlantic, and the other foot in Guam, in the western North Pacific. It has military bases around the world, but these two islands are the farthest outposts of territory actually "owned" by the United States.

## Summary

In January, 1848, gold was discovered at Captain Sutter's sawmill at Coloma, California. Soon after that—and before the news leaked—Mexico ceded California and New Mexico to the United States. Then, with the news of gold's discovery, thousands of people from all parts of the country hurried to California to dig for gold, and so that state grew more rapidly in population than any other new part of the United States ever had in the same length of time. Before the 19th century ended, the United States added the Gadsden Purchase, Alaska, Hawaii, and several other small islands to its territories.

## Questions

Who was Captain Sutter?

Where did he live?

Tell how he lived.

What did he begin to build at Coloma?

Tell what Marshall found there, and what his companions said about it.

What happened when Marshall took the shining dust to Captain Sutter?

What did the captain do?

What made them both certain that the dust was gold?

Was the captain pleased with the discovery?

What did the captain think would happen?

What is said about the United States' war with Mexico?

What did the two countries fight about?

What did the United States get at the end of the war?

What happened in May of 1848? Then what happened?

How many people went to California?

What happened to Captain Sutter?

What is said about Marshall?

What land did the United States buy in 1853?

And what did they buy in 1867?

How long ago did the Revolution end?

How many states did the United States have at that time? And now?

Can you recount:

• What land did the United States buy in 1803?

• In 1819?

• What territory did the Union add in 1845?

• In 1846?

• In 1848?

• 1853?

• 1867?

• And 1898?

• How many such additions has the United States made in all?

Where is the eastern foot of the United States?

And the western foot?

# Index

With pronunciation of difficult words.

The numbers refer to page numbers where the words first appear.

makes treaty with Massasoit, 55–56.

Catholics

treatment in England, 63.

colony in Newfoundland, 63–64.

colony in Maryland, 64–65.

give equal religious rights to Protestants, 65–67.

persecuted in Maryland, 67.

first English Church of, in America, 66.

Charles II. and Penn, 87, 89–90.

Church, Captain Benjamin, 83–84.

Clark, George Rogers, 171–177.

Coloma (Kuh-lo'muh), gold discovered at, 247.

Columbus, 1–14.

Compass

Smith's use of the, 32.

Roger Williams', 71.

Washington's use of, 125.

Concord, battle of, 131.

Congress,

declares independence, 92, 136–137.

makes Washington commander-in-chief, 134.

meaning of word (note), 92, 129.

meeting of the first, 92, 129.

votes money for first telegraph lines, 232–233.

Cornwallis, Lord, in the Revolution, 137–144.

Cotton, 181–182, 184, 187–188.

Cotton gin, 182–185.

Cowpens, battle of, 139–142, 216.

Crockett, David, 239.

Dare, Virginia, birth of, 26.